GOP GPS

GOP GPS

How to Find the Millennials and Urban Voters the Republican Party Needs to Survive

Evan Siegfried

Foreword by Robert A. George

Skyhorse Publishing

Skyhorse Publishing books may be purchased in bulk at special discounts for sales promotion, corporate gifts, fund-raising, or educational purposes. Special editions can also be created to specifications. For details, contact the Special Sales Department, Skyhorse Publishing, 307 West 36th Street, 11th Floor, New York, NY 10018 or info@skyhorsepublishing.com.

Visit our website at www.skyhorsepublishing.com.

10 9 8 7 6 5 4 3 2 1

Library of Congress Cataloging-in-Publication Data is available on file.

Cover design by Rain Saukas
Cover photo credit: AP Images

Print ISBN: 978-1-5107-1732-9
Ebook ISBN: 978-1-5107-1733-6

Printed in the United States of America

For my parents.

Contents

Foreword

NEW AMERICANS

By Robert A. George

April 19, 2016, 11:00 p.m.: Having just finished doing a recap of the Democratic and Republican presidential primaries on New York's twenty-four-hour news station, I stepped into the car waiting for me outside. Settling in, I noticed that the driver was also listening to the results on the radio: both Donald Trump and Hillary Clinton had won their respective primaries fairly easily. I buckled up. Starting up the car, he turned off the radio. I said, "Oh, it's OK. You can leave the radio on."

He said that he just wanted to keep an eye on the primary results while he was waiting for me. It turned out that he closely followed politics. Earlier that day he had gone out and voted for Hillary Clinton. He lived in Valley Stream, Long Island.

Detecting an accent I asked him where he was from. Where had he grown up? Pakistan. His name? Khan. I asked him how long he had been living in the United States. Twenty-seven years. I told him that I had been born in Trinidad and partly grew up in England. At this point, we immediately bonded over cricket—a sport popular in all three countries.

The conversation drifted back to politics. Khan made an observation that I had encountered only too frequently in recent months: "It seems the Republicans don't like the immigrants." I said, it's a bit more complicated than that. Of course, trying for nuance in the era of Trump is a fool's errand.

Khan said, "Last time around," obviously referring to 2012, "Mr. Romney was a very good businessman. He was doing very well, then he started attacking immigrants and he lost support." In fairness, Khan's memory wasn't perfect: back in 2012, Mitt Romney (despite what some Republicans would like to remember) trailed President Obama for most of the campaign. If there was a point when the effort turned fatal, it was most likely after the infamous "47 percent" tape was released.

That said, Khan made an important point. For an immigrant like him, the piercing memory of the 2012 presidential election was that the standard-bearer for the Republican Party had endorsed the notion of "self-deportation" to deal with the immigration problem.

It mattered little that Romney was specifically talking about illegal immigration. It mattered little that he was talking about what to do with undocumented immigrants entering via the Southern border.

In the context of the contemporary media environment, the message relayed was, "Mitt Romney hates immigrants." And it was a message that had disastrous impact: As poorly as the Romney-Ryan ticket did with Hispanic voters (27%), it did even worse with Asians (26%)—a group of which my driver was a proud member.

The Romney results showed quite clearly that, despite very different profiles, Asian and Hispanic immigrants were hearing the same thing from the Republican Party in 2012: you are not welcome.

And, if Khan was any indication, that message was resounding even more broadly in 2016. And why wouldn't it? The GOP's apparent frontrunner, Donald Trump, debuted his campaign with a broadside denouncing illegal immigrants from Mexico. Months later, in the face of terrorist attacks in Europe and California, he doubled down by calling for a general ban on Muslim immigrants "until we can figure out what's going on."

Using the 2012 example, one could only speculate how many other groups—whether explicitly mentioned by Trump or not—will hear the "you're not welcome message" and vote accordingly.

Hasn't the GOP been here before? Wasn't there a much-ballyhooed "autopsy" following the 2012? Yes and yes. RNC Chairman Reince Priebus released a full report after 2012—with recommendations that included the party getting its immigration act together. And the reward for that was the whole enterprise blowing up in the party's face. Senator Marco Rubio took the lead on a bipartisan bill in the Senate. The comprehensive bill became anathema to the GOP base and never went anywhere in the Tea Party–dominated House of Representatives. Worse, Rubio's role helped drag down his presidential aspirations.

So, four years later, the GOP is arguably in even worse shape.

Two weeks after Khan and I had that fascinating conversation, the Republican Party presidential nomination process came to an abrupt and screeching halt: the Indiana primary confirmed what the prior New York and "Acela" (Northeastern) contests implied: It was Donald Trump's Republican Party and Donald and Hillary's political world. For many—especially on the GOP side—these are nothing but depressing prospects.

But all is not lost. To the contrary, one could argue that the presumptive Donald/Hillary nominations are the last gasps of a culture war that has raged for decades. At sixty-eight and seventy, Clinton and Trump would be the oldest combined-age presidential candidates—ever. They will also most likely be the last baby boomers to lead their parties (please, let it be).

In 2016, Trump and Clinton are barely candidates. Rather, they are avatars of their respective side of the culture war—Trump, the fire-breathing, unapologetic white alpha male; Clinton, the ascendant identity-conscious Social Justice-Warrior. As representatives of the dominant cultural generation for five decades and the political one for two-and-a-half, these boomers limp to a last presidential election absent ideas—full of sound and fury, signifying . . . what exactly?

It may turn out that the long-term change is better coming from an outsider—an unelected observer—than from current party leaders, elected or otherwise.

Which is why Evan Siegfried's message comes along at the ideal time.

Seriously? What can a thirty-something white guy say to the Republican Party that it hasn't heard before?

Well, in truth, regardless of what happens in 2016, the Republican Party—loser of the popular vote in five of the last six presidential elections—needs a new message for the twenty-first century. Yes, lightning *could* strike and the GOP could capture the White House (though, as of late spring that seems unlikely). However, it's been an unpredictable election cycle: Hillary Clinton *could* face legal problems; the economy *could* take a downturn, which would give Trump's dour anti-immigrant, anti-free trade, message a general election resonance.

But even if all of those things happen, the underlying demographic trends shaping the nation and the electorate won't change in the long-run, one election aside—even if, say, a President Trump manages to curtail the number of immigrants coming in (which he won't).

Evan Siegfried zeroes in on the urban dweller for a simple, yet very important reason: he's a Republican and these are his neighbors. Cities are magnets that draw young people, immigrants, and religious and ethnic minorities of all backgrounds. Not coincidentally, these are the very same groups that the Republican Party has had difficulty reaching in recent elections. Or, better yet, these are the groups that—as Khan exemplifies—no longer wish to give the GOP the time of day.

In short, in an America that is constantly reinventing itself, cities are Ground Zero. After years of decline, cities—urban centers—have seen a revival over the last few decades. More Americans are flocking to cities and those huge population centers carry an outsized influence in states.

As the *Washington Post* reported on March 27, 2014:

> New Census data released this year suggests that within the last year (from July 1, 2012, to July 1, 2013), virtually all of the country's population growth took place in metropolitan areas, with a significant chunk of it even further clustered in and around the largest cities. Over that year, the number of people living in metropolitan America increased by 2.3 million, a figure that reflects both natural growth and in-migration. The population in what the Census calls "micropolitan statistical areas"—smaller population centers with a core of fewer than 50,000 people—grew by a mere 8,000 souls.

Meanwhile, in 2016, millennials surpassed boomers as the nation's largest generation. So, as the boomers have their last gasp at the presidency, two generations behind them is a rising group that requires *its* needs to be addressed—and it's more than just student loans.

Siegfried comes to the table with these stats and surveys and a heckuva lot more. A native New Yorker, he lives and breathes the urban existence. He's more than comfortable living in a diverse cosmopolitan environment. But, having grown up in a liberal city, he knows what works in the contemporary urban setting and what doesn't. He's seen New York governed by Rudy Giuliani, Michael Bloomberg, and now Bill de Blasio. The results speak for themselves—especially on education and policing.

On those issues alone, urban and rural Republicans have much in common. It's the basic common-sense viewpoint that, on schools, the old top-down public school paradigm no longer works. In an era where babies are born into a world as digital natives and take to an iPhone like playing with building blocks, our education system is seriously outmoded. The party willing to encourage alternative education methods across the board will capture the twenty-first century. A Democratic Party unwilling to distance itself from the teachers union is ill-equipped to do that.

Urban politicians—including Republicans—tend to believe more in gun-use regulation than do their peers across the country. As a result, someone like a Michael Bloomberg is anathema to Republicans in the South and the heartland. But it doesn't have to always be that way. Sure, Rudy Giuliani didn't go anywhere when he ran for president. That sure doesn't mean that his tough get-things-done message doesn't translate elsewhere.

Evan Siegfried has seen that, too, and realizes that there are better solutions—and Republicans can find them and articulate them for urban audiences if they're only willing to do the work. As one of the older millennials himself, Evan stands at the generational nexus. He's seen what the boomers have done to his country, but he's more than comfortable enough with the technology that has made it much easier to communicate, educate, and entertain diverse audiences. Ultimately, this is how post-Trump Republicans will have to identify and build their new constituencies. What the millennial, the immigrant, and the general urban dweller have in common is that they're hiding in plain sight. They have their own language(s), culture(s), and dwelling(s).

They're open to new takes on old problems—if you (the politician) are willing to see them as they are. Are you willing to withhold judgment? Refrain from imposing your views on them? Well, they may give you a hearing.

My mind drifts back to my driver Khan—a hard-working man from Pakistan. A man who had respect for the Republican Party's previous presidential nominee—until Romney (in Khan's view) decided to go after immigrants. Seeing how the 2016 campaign's evident standard-bearer has already put his stamp on the party, this year's GOP has already lost Khan.

I learned a lot from a short car ride from New York's Chelsea Market area up to my home in Washington Heights. Readers of this book are going to learn a whole lot more—about politics, ideas, and even a little bit about Evan's love life. More importantly, you'll learn about a Republican Party that you might not have realized even existed (or, as described by Evan, that you perhaps might want to join).

Just sit back and take in the sober (well, most of the time) analyses of one smart young man. He's got a lot to share, and does so in a smooth conversational manner, avoiding most jargon, using anecdotes and up-to-the-moment stats to make his point.

The next four years will be a time of great soul-searching for a Republican Party desperate to make itself attractive to the newest Americans. Evan Siegfried's already got a leg up on how to go about that.

May as well join him for the ride.

Introduction

The night was going well. My idea for wine at a fun downtown New York City bar was a hit. My date was an attractive and accomplished second-year associate corporate litigator at a fairly well-known law firm who possessed a smile that portrayed a level of kindness most New Yorkers aren't believed to be capable of having.

"I am a Republican."

My date's face slowly changed from smile to confusion, as she began to wrap her head around what I had just said. The mood and trajectory of the evening changed as, with those four words, what had been a promising first date became a quasi-interrogation. I was on the defensive and she morphed from potential paramour to grand inquisitor.

The questions came fast and furious on issues, mainly social, that my answers only sowed further confusion. Do I believe that gays should not be allowed to marry and be treated equally under the law? That we should have a national database of people who are of the Muslim faith? Why don't I respect the right of a woman to choose whether or not she terminates a pregnancy? What is up with pushing economic policies that cater to the 1 percent? Why don't I recognize the problems and threats of global warming? How come I don't want to help minorities? What's with the constant admiring references to President Reagan?

To my date, by merely admitting my Republican voter registration status, I instantly morphed into the caricature that the left and the media have created of those on the right.

She finished her well-meaning, rapid-fire rhetorical questions and I prepared to answer them as best I could—of course, after taking a rather generous sip of wine. After all, how could someone who is pro–marriage equality and a believer in climate change be, in her eyes, so backward?

This book seeks not only to explain that Republicans are far from backward, but that they are more than the reflexive caricature that my date and many others have come to view us as. Further, it seeks to assess where we are as a party in our ideas and offer solutions for challenges that await us, particularly ones that impact our ability to grow and sustain for decades to come.

I am absolutely certain that some people will call me crazy for suggesting that we Republicans can bring millennials and urban residents to our party. It is not that they are opposed to expanding the GOP with these groups, but rather they feel it is a losing battle. They like to say that liberals and Democrats never convert to our side, especially if they come from heavily "blue" strongholds. This would be a good argument, were it true.

Perhaps it is time that I confess something about myself. It is a deep and dark secret that only my friends and family know. I am not proud to admit it, but I was once a registered Democrat. I am quite aware of the stigma that comes with it. Yes, I am a bit of a leper and figure marked for scorn. However, I am also living proof that Democrats who are both millennials and urban voters can be become Republicans if they are convinced the right way.

My own journey to the Republican Party and conservatism is unusual. Who would expect a New Yorker who grew up on Manhattan's Upper West Side, the bastion of liberalism that gave rise to the term "liberal New Yorker," that is half-Jewish and half-Christian, to become a Republican?! Nobody. The mainly white neighborhood that I grew up in was a haven for Democrats; Republicans were less common than homeless people on the street corner.

To me and the kids I grew up with, the government was an institution built for doing good and automatically trusted without question. We were taught that if we were ever in trouble or needed help, we were to seek out the nearest police officer or firefighter. They were there to protect us. So it was only natural that the government itself was viewed as an extension of the goodness and safety of its employees. This was in the era when New York City was being run by Democratic mayors Ed Koch and David Dinkins. I can still remember the mayoral election of 1993 when Republican Rudy Giuliani took on the incumbent Dinkins and asked New Yorkers if they felt safe. They did not and Giuliani was ushered into office.

Suddenly, a Republican was manning the helm of New York City government and showing himself to be anything but the disaster Democrats painted him to be. In fact, because of Rudy Giuliani's two terms as mayor of the city of New York, New York restored its lost glory, increased its prosperity, and returned from the brink. Citizens did not need to fear being robbed, raped, or murdered because they walked down the street at the wrong time of day. They saw that conservative ideals and policies could make the world in which they lived a better place. (Although some Democrats today will still deny this fact.)

Despite the success of Mayor Giuliani, I remained a Democrat. Republicans were suffering locally because of the stereotype that national conservatives created for them. By the time I was old enough to register to vote, I chose the Democratic Party because that is what New Yorkers did. Checking the GOP box on the voter registration form would have been inviting mockery and made me somewhat of an outcast. Nobody, especially when they are a teenager, wants to be subjected to those things.

Soon, it became clear to me that local Democrats were far from honest. They were the product of political machines that existed solely to perpetuate their own grip on power. Election Day saw every Democratic nominee win their local race. The true electoral contests took place in the Democratic primaries. For me, primaries became more about voting against a particular candidate more than voting for one. Such was (and is) the slate of utterly uninspiring or qualified Democrats offered up each election. It was part of the recipe that made me convert.

After boarding school in Maine, college at Fordham University, working for the United Nations, US Senate, and former Mayor Giuliani's 2008 presidential campaign, I entered government service with the intention of doing some good without being in a political position. Working in the clerk's office of the United States District Court for the Eastern District of New York exposed me to the best and worst of government and its employees. The judges and their law clerks exemplified what good government could be. They brought an excitement, professionalism, and efficiency that every public servant should strive to achieve. However, this was in stark contrast to the majority of the employees (who were not attorneys) in the courthouse. Like me, presumptively, most entered government service seeking to do some good for the United States and its citizens. They entered a system resistant to change. It allowed employees to "fail up," while stifling success. Every action you took was chronicled and recorded. The times when I found a way to make things better, I was essentially told to not rock the boat. Even more baffling was how competence was rewarded.

If you did a good and efficient job, often you would find your only reward was more work—sometimes this was the work of other employees who had delayed doing it for strategic reasons. At the same time, less responsible or efficient coworkers wound up receiving less work and higher salaries. The message was to keep your head down, do your work (but not too quickly), and you would have a stable and secure income. In some cases, up to twenty workers were doing a job that three competent and motivated workers could do. This was not just the situation in my office, but spread throughout the ranks of the massive federal bureaucracy.

I had to make the most of my time in the Court. Within the building were some of the finest legal minds in the country who were involved in some of the most important federal criminal and civil cases in the United States. I took the advice of a colleague who had become a mentor, who suggested following some cases from start to finish. I was soon paying attention to mob, terrorism, narcotics, and other criminal cases. Without paying an annual tuition of more than $40,000, my time in the Court earned me the equivalent of a master's degree in the federal justice system.

During this time, I continued to expand my understanding of policies and politics. Twitter was rising to prominence in 2008 and 2009. It was how I got my political fix and learned in detail about policies on both sides of the aisle. I wanted to know what drove the people I disagreed with and why they had come to their beliefs. Soon, I found myself nodding in agreement as these conservatives explained their positions and why they held them. I quickly felt like a rube, having bought what the left and the media had been telling me about conservatives for decades. Their ideas were actually really, really good and not the bad policies we had been told they were. Of course, it was also a great help that these conservatives with whom I engaged did more than just talk about politics. We shared common interests from hockey (I mercilessly teased one about being a Red Wings fan) to TV shows and these helped to create more understanding and tolerance for differing views.

I had seen firsthand the myriad of problems that a large government created and presented to the American people. The waste of taxpayer dollars appalled me. If this were a business, it would have folded many times over. How could we allow a system such as this to perpetuate, when it was clear that it was in need of reform? The bureaucracy had even established rules that protected itself from change. This protection came in the form of how business was conducted and how employees could be let go (the joke was once you were hired, you would basically have to be convicted of murder in order to be fired).

There is nothing wrong with people, including liberals, wanting government to be a positive force in people's lives, but government clearly is incapable of doing so when it operates in this manner. Adding to the challenges of government running effectively are the many rules it uses to self-govern. Change is virtually impossible because of them. Government is bloated and broken.

In my heart I knew I was no longer a Democrat, but, ironically, I had a real problem changing my registration. Government "efficiency" prevented me from changing my registration for over a year. I would log onto the New York State DMV website, change my registration from D to R and then discover months later that the system had not registered the change due to some technical glitch. After my third attempt, I did what most millennials are loath to do; I filed a paper registration change and used the United States Postal Service to deliver it. Finally, my long journey to the ranks of the GOP and conservatism was complete.

After I felt ready to "come out of the closet" so to speak, I emailed a conservative friend of mine that I had met through Twitter. I told her that I had finally become a Republican after realizing that I was a conservative. I expected that she would respond with congratulations. I was pleasantly surprised and could not help but chuckle when she wrote back, "Most unsurprising news of the century :) Mazel!" She knew that this urban millennial was not a Democrat, but a Republican who needed a little bit of coaxing combined with the right set of circumstances to find his true political identity.

I suspect that I am not the only millennial or urban voter who could embrace conservatism, as well as the Republican Party. Among my own friends that are not inside the political arena, most are liberal, but when we do discuss politics, many find themselves agreeing with the conservative ideas and principles I put forth. They do so not because I'm some great orator—I'm not—but rather because I present my argument in a method that is based in fact and logic, while being delivered via a medium with which they are comfortable engaging. Millennials and urban voters shall be the dominant and deciding voters of the twenty-first century. To ignore them and not bring them into the fold is outright political malpractice. Every single recommendation provided throughout this book will be geared toward them. These ideas might not appeal or necessarily work in more rural areas or with older generations. Nonetheless, millennials and urban voters are the future of the American electorate and should be invested in now so as to avoid having to play a daunting and expensive game of catch-up later. Think of it this way: millennials are the company Google when it debuted on the stock market in 2004 for just under $50 a share. Today, Google's stock prices have soared to over $700 a share. Would you prefer to invest in the company now or 2004? The Republican Party faces that same question, but the only difference is that we are able to ask this question when it is essentially 2004 (i.e., it will cost less to attract millennials now than it would in ten or fifteen years).

Millennials are now becoming disenfranchised with both the Democratic and Republican Parties. Almost half of them identify as independent and are not a member of either side of the political aisle. They hold the view that our political system is broken and are not turning out to vote at the same rate other generations are. It isn't because of political apathy, but due to how they do not feel particularly connected.

> In the 2014 midterm elections, the turnout among millennials didn't match that of other age groups—a typical pattern with young voters. Moreover, Democrats didn't win as large a percentage of them as two years earlier.[1]

This tidbit from a February 2016 *Wall Street Journal* report is actually a promising opportunity. While Republicans are having trouble connecting with millennials, so too are Democrats. That is a bit of good news for the GOP. However, let's remember that Democrats are not sitting idly by, throwing their hands in the air and letting this happen. The Democratic Party is furiously attempting to reverse what appears to be a decline among millennials.

As far as urban residents are concerned, it is going to be a tougher slog for Republicans. We at the Grand Old Party are primarily culpable and should be held accountable for our decline in urban areas. It's a problem of our own making and now we need to be responsible and fix it. Doing so will open up many more paths to victory in elections to come.

Congressman Justin Amash (R-Michigan) was earnest when he told a February 2016 audience at the Heritage Foundation's monthly *Conversations with Conservatives* that:

> What's been missing on the Republican side is reaching out to the black community. I think it's important that we do more of that as a party, because we do have a lot to offer everyone. We're about individual liberty and opportunity. This top-down, government-centered model has not worked for communities throughout our country.[2]

However, the fact that Congressman Amash said this truism changes absolutely nothing and doesn't move the needle in favor of Republicans in urban areas. In fact, it earned Amash and the other attendees of this particular *Conversations with Conservatives* condemnation by the left and media. It was framed as another example of Republicans being out of touch with urban voters. If anything, it hardened resistance to the GOP in urban and minority communities. Even though it is true, just saying it won't achieve results. What will achieve results is a program that backs up our words with actions on policies, and highlighting Democratic failure with these ethnic groups and communities.

The content outlined in this tome is not necessarily something that is a blanket prescription for the Republican Party. Instead, it should be viewed as a surgical one for urban areas such as New York

City, Chicago, Los Angeles, and other cities that have been dominated by Democrats and their failed policies. For example, when it comes to guns, New York City has an entirely different set of circumstances and beliefs than Boise, Idaho. Each locality has its own set of conditions that requires its own unique approach. What works in New York does not necessarily work in Boise and vice versa. Yes, there are some suggestions that are made that should be adopted nationally. These mostly pertain to issues of equality and civil rights, as they are ones that adhere to how an individual is treated and ultimately come down to matters of basic fairness. The government does not have the right to discriminate against any person for any reason, as all citizens are viewed as equal under the law. This is an example of the federal government providing a broad set of basic rules to which all local governments are required to adhere. Issues such as the Second Amendment, on the other hand, are not ones that should be decided at the federal level. The very definition of conservatism calls for the local government to determine its own laws, but to do so by using the aforementioned broad definition of how a government can treat its citizens. Boise has the right to enact a law that its citizens can walk down the street with a pistol strapped to their leg. This law applies to every person, no matter their race, color, sexuality, or faith. At the same time, New York City has the right to say that its gun-owning citizens cannot walk down the street with a firearm unless they have obtained a special permit. Agree with these laws or not, we cannot violate a person's rights, especially ones afforded them under the Fourteenth Amendment's Equal Protection Clause. We, the Republican Party, are entitled to differing views and debate across the country. It's what gives us diversity and rich ideas worth discussing.

Polls and surveys shall also be used to fortify arguments that are set forth in this book. Yet, I must also add the caveat that polls are a brief snapshot in time. Public opinion often shifts, especially in response to events that might not be foreseen. Democrats (and Republicans) quite often cite this fact when confronted with evidence of how the public does not agree them on an issue or in a campaign. What does make polling numbers more concrete is when a series of polls demonstrate a trend. When presenting polling results, every attempt will be made to do so using sets of data that clearly show and demonstrate the public mood on whatever matter is being discussed.

The Republican Party is in a state of limbo and its future is not set. All of its major factions have finally broken from one another, as the circumstances and figures holding it together could no longer be kept from trying to become ruling ideology within the party. 2016's presidential nominating contest has revealed that Republicans are now viewed as a damaged brand that is lacking a coherent vision and identity. The division and strife within the Republican Party has made many openly wonder if the party of Lincoln will exist in the next decade.

Where we go in the future will be debated to no end. Some will call for us to be as conservative as possible and never compromise on any issue. This idea was pushed previously in 2008 and 2012 after John McCain and Mitt Romney failed to win the presidency in their respective elections. The people pushing their failure neglect to take into account the overwhelming evidence that extreme conservatism without flexibility only alienates the Republican Party from most Americans. They willfully ignore the mountain of evidence that shows that when people are too intractably conservative, voters will reject them. Pushing for rigid purity within the GOP is the gradual path to extinction.

However, taking stock of who, what, and where we are as a major political party in the United States, followed by charting a sound course toward the future, will ensure the Republican Party's survival. Our ability to continue and function as a dominant major party in the United States is our shared common goal.

No, I do not have all of the answers, nor should I. Any person who claims to have all the answers is more than likely selling snake oil. Approach them with great caution and skepticism. In reality,

I'm just a guy who cares about the future of the Republican Party and is offering a solution and road map to some of the hurdles we face both presently and in the future.

Some within the Republican Party will assuredly accuse me of being a heretic and RINO (Republican In Name Only). Let them. Chances are these are not people who are going to be willing to listen to advice from me, or from anybody else for that matter, about how the GOP needs to evolve to survive. They adhere to a strict orthodoxy that is exactly what is hurting our great party.

At the same time, many on the left will think me some sort of preachy and patronizing conservative who is lecturing them about what is good for them. They are already primed to believe that many conservatives want to tell them how they should live their lives, particularly on matters of reproductive rights and religion. Perhaps they will even say that I am trying to exploit them by suckering them into voting for GOP candidates so that the Republican Party can remain in power and pursue its "secret agenda of keeping the poor man down" or something. Whatever.

While writing this, a friend told me that I was tilting at windmills when it came to trying to convert some of these groups, particularly Black Lives Matter and other protest movements. She told me they're too close-minded and inflexible when it comes to alternative ideas. Maybe, but there are members of these movements who would be open to new ideas if the ideas were presented in a proper manner. We're not going to win all of them over, but we still must try. We must win over some that are a part of these social justice movements, as well as those who aren't involved in them. It is important that we try or else we will face dire consequences at the ballot box.

As I wrote this book, I had many conversations with friends and colleagues about the issues. The common concern that they had was how receptive would Republicans be to hear that they must change? Each time, my answer was the same: think of the Republican Party as a product and you are in charge of selling it. If the product isn't selling and you are having diminishing returns, you don't stay the course! You figure out ways to improve and upgrade the product to suit the market, but don't do so in a way that the product loses its core identity. Republicans can and must take positions that are more in line with the beliefs of voters, but that still adhere to our conservative values. Evolving is not a betrayal of our beliefs, but a natural growth over time.

This book is part of a larger conversation that Republicans need to have. Millennials and urban voters are quickly becoming the future of the American electorate and the GOP isn't an appealing political choice for them. We have been able to do without them, and they without us, in election cycles past, but now we are facing a future where they will be large enough and powerful enough to relegate us to being the minority party for years upon years. That is just one estimate that paints a best-case scenario situation. Other outcomes see this lasting for decades or even the total dissolution of the Republican Party itself. None of these end results are outcomes that neither I nor any other member of the GOP should want to face. Instead, we must work to ensure that these realities never happen.

I know I am the minority, as I am both a millennial and an urban resident. I grew up in heavily Democratic New York City (where I still live) and have watched the Republican brand become tarnished firsthand. My parents were both rather liberal growing up (granted my dad became more conservative after I became an adult) and so were the communities that I was a part of. Yet, I ultimately became a Republican. It wasn't out of some sort of desire to revolt, but rather a realization that conservatives were far better on the issues than liberals. If I can come to this conclusion, then so can many millennials and urban residents. They just need the proper enticement and support structures to join the GOP.

Let's face it; this book also opens me up to charges that I wrote this for selfish reasons. I admit it—I did write this for my own benefit: I want to be able to go on dates without ever having to defend my political beliefs. I would rather spend my time and energy arguing over what to watch on Netflix and order for dinner.

Chapter 1
What a caricature we are now

THERE IS THE STORY OF THE FORMER ROMAN GENERAL, LUCIUS Quinctius Cincinnatus. Cincinnatus had been a general in the Roman army and a consul of Rome, but retired in shame after one of his sons had been tried in absentia and sentenced to death. He worked on a small farm removed from public life, when in 458 BC the man became a legend. Rome was under the threat of invasion by the Aequi and the Sabines. With Rome in a state of crisis, the consul of Rome nominated Cincinnatus to quell the threat by serving as dictator. The position was one of absolute power and held no accountability. If he wanted to, Cincinnatus could seize power for life, and Rome would have no legal recourse to remove him from control of the Roman Empire. Instead, he set out with the Roman army and neutralized the threat of the Sabines and Aequi. After doing so, Cincinnatus surrendered his unlimited power and returned to his farm to lead a quiet life. He had been dictator for a total of fifteen days.

In 439 BC, Rome called Cincinnatus out of retirement once again when Spurius Maelius and several others sought to seize power via a coup and install Maelius as king. Cincinnatus returned to the position of dictator to pacify this internal threat to Rome and did so quickly. Maelius was killed when Cincinnatus's second in command went to arrest him, and his coconspirators soon had a change of heart about the coup. As he had before, Cincinnatus relinquished his power and returned to private life on his farm. He died at the age of eighty-nine in 430 BC.

Almost 2,500 years after he lived, the example of Cincinnatus is often cited as the truest devotion to civic virtue. Here we have a man who not once, but twice, achieved ultimate power and surrendered it as quickly as possible. He knew that holding power for too long can corrupt and lead most people to betray their ideals. The comfort and thrill of power often entices us to shout down our better angels. It is why we have seen our elected leaders gain office as self-professed devotees of civic virtue and, assuming they ever leave office, rarely exit elected office as devoted to civic virtue as they first were.

Both Republicans and Democrats are guilty of trying to hold onto whatever power and influence their offices grant them. They use their positions to advance and solidify their status as elected officials through gerrymandering, legislative giveaways, and slick public relations strategies. Every step they take is designed with one goal in mind: to remain in power. This is exactly why Americans today feel so strongly that our elected federal officials are not there to serve the people, but themselves. This certainly contributes to how the country overwhelmingly believes that Washington is broken. The example of Cincinnatus is not a reason that we should have term limits for legislators (that's an entirely different debate), but a good reminder of how our leaders should behave. He was famous for giving up absolute power, but if you look at his overall career, you will find other things to admire. He pushed his agenda for, as the Romans called it, the "glory of Rome" and not the glory of Cincinnatus. Many of our elected officials and leaders profess they are there to help the United States, but are there to really help themselves. This is not new (history is filled with people who have sought to use their positions to make gains) and will continue throughout the course of human history. It's in our nature. However, there are those who do seek office for the right reasons and they should be celebrated. Unfortunately, when we debate the issues of the day, each side attempts to portray the opposition as somehow self-serving and seeking to hold onto power at all costs. It's a public relations strategy that only impacts us for the worse.

The goal of many elected officials is to never cede power and to hold onto it at all costs. They are the polar opposite of Cincinnatus. There can be no debate that power is a drug that gives those who hold it the ultimate high. Power begets money. Power begets success. Power begets influence. If shown the path to power, who among us would not deign or endeavor to walk such a road? Once on it, they need to keep in a constant state of forward progress while leaving those that seek to take their place behind. It is why many politicians and leaders will fight to the bitter end in order to maintain their advance on the path of power.

The public relations strategies employed by politicians seek to pit one side against the other on each and every issue. Both sides of the aisle seek to claim the moral high ground in whatever debate they are engaged in and make their opposition's point of view unpalatable to the public. Part of this has involved dumbing down the conversation and making the public believe that the word "intellectual" holds a negative connotation. Republicans in particular are guilty of this crime, as we have used this line against opponents. Sarah Palin and others have also railed against "elites" of the party. They spin the yarn that these "elites" and the amorphous "establishment" are against the common man and are pursuing some secretive agenda to benefit themselves. It is really just a way for these people to hide their own shortcomings. They cannot win an argument based on facts and reason, so they must whip up their supporters into a state of anger and then tell them who to blame. People do not like others who believe themselves smarter than they are. So why not just accuse all who display intelligence or are doing something they do not like of being snooty? It's a useful political tool, but serves no real purpose in advancing discourse.

To the Palins of the world, to think deeply is somehow to err and be deserving of scorn. Since when has being an intellectual truly been something to ridicule?! Don't Americans want to be intellectual? Don't parents hope that their children will grow up to be intellectual? This makes no sense and is actually a hindrance to the arguments that Republicans seek to make with the American people. The way we Republicans will win over new voters is through using intellectual arguments, not by calling others names or hurling insults.

Name-calling and mudslinging only backfire when it comes to winning over people. Sure, it is red meat for the base (as the presidential campaign of Donald Trump has demonstrated), as it fires them up over whatever issue is at hand. Yet, the base is already supporting us, whereas the swing opinion voters have yet to make up their minds as to what side of the argument that they will fall on. Attacks only push us apart. Now, if we took the approach that debates over issues and policy were to be fought with well-reasoned, rational, and fact-based logic, then Americans would listen.

The presidential campaign of Donald Trump would be a natural rebuttal to the recommendation that Republicans use calm and sensible arguments in order to win a debate. Sure, his bombastic style gave him the lead from the start of his campaign in June 2015 right through Super Tuesday and on. Trump's rhetoric only turned off independent voters from the Republican Party and damaged Republicans across the United States. The people who like this stream of insults are not the people that the GOP needs to target in order to grow. We already have many of them in the fold, although their support of Trump shows their dissatisfaction with how Republicans (and Democrats) have governed of late.

The dissatisfaction of the Trump supporters was warranted. For years, they had dealt with politicians who had overpromised and under-delivered. George W. Bush and other Republicans professed their fiscal conservative "credentials" and "values," but when push came to shove, they presided over a massive increase in federal spending, with it rising 60 percent over the course of Bush's presidency.[3] In 2008, Barack Obama campaigned on bringing America and its people "hope" and "change." Yet, after he took office and when it came time for the rubber to meet the road, nothing happened. Some proposals and initiatives became law, but their impact was not felt by the people. Some of these laws and initiatives actually made their lives harder. Take the American Recovery and Reinvestment Act of 2009 (more commonly known as "the stimulus package"). It sought to use public funds to offset the massive decline in private spending due to the Great Recession and foster an economically healthy climate. Few citizens saw any direct impact of the $831 billion of this public spending. Then there is the Affordable Care Act, a.k.a Obamacare, which has driven the prices of insurance up and made it harder for all Americans to have access to quality health care. Obama promised hope and change, but brought gridlock and partisan discord. Citizens' outrage is perfectly reasonable and understandable.

So when a candidate who exudes success (or at least markets themselves to be successful despite evidence to the contrary) like Donald Trump comes along, they are willing to listen. He's not a creature of Washington, and he already had the name recognition because of his reality show, *The Apprentice*, and by saying what he felt. Trump himself was the perfect vehicle for their justifiable anger. Trump would attack anyone and everyone he could, and his supporters loved it. The attacks could be incredibly inappropriate and his backers would defend Trump with the phrase, "But he fights!" This was a reference to how they felt that our political leaders surrendered in political fights and, as a result, were somehow weak. Opponents (and sane people) would either attack or condemn the statements, and this had the impact of only hardening support for Trump. "The Donald" was the living embodiment of the term "antifragile," which means something that is resilient, and is strengthened by things that would ordinarily cause a negative impact. It was coined by Professor Nassim Taleb in his 2012 book *Antifragile*. Donald Trump is the antifragile candidate and it's a completely new phenomenon for many of us operatives to deal with.

Through many conversations with Trump supporters over the course of writing this book, a common theme emerged. These people, many of whom were decent and fairly normal citizens, felt that all that the government and its leaders had done for them was just take, take, and take. They did not feel like the government was giving them a single thing. They knew Trump was vulgar, thin-skinned, lacked the judgment required to be president, had a history of business failures, and generally was not qualified to sit in the Oval Office. Yet, they supported him regardless. The feeling that the government had subjected them to abuse, be it real or imagined, was palpable in these conversations. To them, the federal government took from them and gave nothing in exchange. Further, the "establishment," as Trump supporters referred to those in power, had forgotten the example and lesson of Cincinnatus. These Americans wanted to see the whole thing burned to the ground, and Donald Trump was the candidate who would take a flamethrower to the system.

At the same time, the Democratic Party had their own candidate of anger: Senator Bernie Sanders of Vermont. In truth, Sanders was to the left of mainstream Democrats, but solidly in line with the left's angry base. His campaign was based entirely on the issue of income inequality. Sanders raged against wealth stagnation, the power and influence of banks and corporations in our political world, and on and on and on. Like Trump, Sanders was an outsider. He had never really been a part of the Democratic Party and had only joined them in preparation for his 2016 presidential run. In fact, Sanders proudly described himself as a socialist and he didn't stop doing so when he was running for president. You have to admire the man for sticking to his convictions, even when they could be politically inconvenient.

Both Donald Trump and Bernie Sanders used rhetoric on the campaign trail that incited passion among their supporters and antagonized opponents. Trump would often launch tirades, both in public appearances and on Twitter, which would demean whoever was the target of his ire. Frequently used taunts were "loser" or "nobody likes them" or "sad" or "fired, like a dog" (this begs the question of what exactly does that mean?!). And then there were the nicknames: "Lyin Ted" or "Little Marco," or "Crooked Hillary," and even "Goofy Elizabeth Warren" (whom he actually called "Pocahontas)." When it came to television personalities or media outlets, he would accuse them of having provided no journalism or having low ratings or circulation. It was quite obviously presidential.

The Sanders rhetoric was less pointed but equally passionate. He often used terms that encouraged class warfare. Meredith Warren called out Sanders and Democrats in an editorial in the *Boston Globe* in September 2015:

> For years, Democrats have used an economic inequality argument to attract voters to their cause and pit certain groups of Americans against others. But they go beyond just making intellectual policy points. It's a call to arms in a class war they are trying to incite for their own political gain.[4]

Warren further explained that it was Sanders himself who directly called it a war when he wrote in a July 2015 editorial, also in the *Boston Globe*:

> It is time to say loudly and clearly that corporate greed and the war against the American middle class must end. Enough is enough![5]

Calling this a war against the middle class is completely inappropriate and wrong. Republicans and the left just disagree on how to achieve economic equality. Bernie Sanders knows this and despite this knowledge, exploits this for political gain. And he's not the only Democrat who does this.

Take Congressman Alan Grayson (D-Florida) who has a penchant for making patently absurd statements. In 2009, during the debate over Obamacare, he said the following of Republicans:

> It's my duty and pride tonight to be able to announce exactly what the Republicans plan to do for health care in America . . . It's a very simple plan. Here it is. The Republican health-care plan for America: "Don't get sick." If you have insurance, don't get sick; if you don't have insurance, don't get sick; if you're sick, don't get sick. Just don't get sick. . . . If you do get sick America, the Republican health-care plan is this: die quickly.[6]

Of course, other Democrats did not condemn or refute these crazy remarks. They didn't set the record straight that Republicans did not have a plan to kill Americans who got sick. Conservatives were justifiably upset, but the media ran interference for Grayson and the Democrats. They swept Grayson's words under the rug and barely reported on it. You can bet that if it were a Republican who had said this about Democrats, then it would be the lead story on the nightly news. Then, when Republicans attempted to bring Grayson's statement up as an example of how some Democrats were dealing with Republicans, many on the left and in the media almost mockingly said, "Those crazy Republicans, being upset about a Democratic congressman talking about their health-care plan!" Yup, the Democrats and the Democratic Party condoned this behavior.

Republicans are not without their own crazy-spewing members of the party, too. Ours help to perpetuate the myth of the "out-of-touch Republican" who embodies the caricature created by the left and mainstream media. In 2015, Republican presidential candidate Dr. Ben Carson said that homosexuality was a choice: "People who go into prison, go into prison straight—and when they come out, they're gay."[7]

It was roundly mocked and slammed by the left and other rational groups (as it deserved to be). However, Democrats immediately set out to link Dr. Carson's misguided statement as being a view that all Republicans share. That simply is not true. Why he said it is anybody's guess, but some have speculated that it was because the statement held appeal to a certain sect of the GOP base that believes homosexuality is a lifestyle choice. The argument that Dr. Carson said this to endear himself to this particular portion of Republican voters is plausible.

Another way in which elected officials keep themselves in office is through gerrymandering. When the opportunity to draw congressional districts comes, Republicans and Democrats both seek to draw their congressional districts to their own benefit. This means that they will use census and voter registration data to determine how to carve up their state in order to make a congressional district secure for their own party. Oddly, this practice has unified elected Republicans and Democrats who compromise and agree to split the state's congressional districts a certain way.

It is no surprise that the increase in gerrymandering has coincided with the increase in partisanship and the inability of our elected officials to work together. Correlation does not imply causation in this instance, but there is anecdotal evidence to support the relationship between the two. Districts that are drawn to protect one party's grip on it do not help Americans to have the best elected representatives.

Every two years, American voters have the ability to throw out every single member of the United States House of Representatives, all 435 of them. They do so not through violence or protests, but through casting their vote. Yet because of how congressional districts have been drawn, less than 10 percent of all races for the House of Representatives are even remotely competitive. As a result, we are given elected representatives who might, when first elected, have great and new ideas, but because they are safe from being voted out of office every subsequent election, they face no pressure to amend their policies and views to suit the time. It is important to point out and highlight how gerrymandering does not just occur at the federal level, but it also happens at the local level.

Since they avoid the threat of ouster, they can hold power without changing their views. A clear example of this is seen in New York City, where Democrats have had a monopoly on most elected offices. There is a notable exception: the office of mayor of New York was held by Republicans Rudy Giuliani and Michael Bloomberg from 1994 through 2013. Giuliani was elected following New York's slide into the abyss. Bloomberg was able to use his vast personal wealth to spend his way to election, and in his third term achieved a rather narrow victory despite spending over $100 million of his own money. This level of sheer dominance by Democrats has deprived New York City of a true debate and dialogue on how it should move forward. Now, Democratic policies, many of them harmful, are running rampant and there is nary an opposition.

Chapter 2

We would meet in phone booths (if they still existed)

Being a Republican in New York City, or any big city for that matter, is a bit of a novel thing. Without a doubt, we are a minority and an endangered species. At the end of 2015, for every one of us there were seven Democrats, and the registration gap is growing. Democrats number 3.2 million city residents while Republicans are a mere 470,000. The party has been dwindling and shrinking as the Democratic Party has increased its registration advantage over us.

Since 1992, Republicans have not seriously competed for New York's twenty-nine electoral votes, a sizable number. Each presidential election, the Republican Party and its nominee effectively cede the state to the Democrats. The last time a Republican presidential nominee won New York State?—1984. We have not had a statewide-elected Republican since 2006 with Governor George Pataki and he last won a statewide election in 2002.

Why has New York become so blue that it cannot elect a Republican to statewide office?

To many New Yorkers, particularly in New York City, the Republican brand is tarnished. It has lurched too far to the right on social issues and become too radical. Such views make it hard for Republicans to be elected within New York City, as voters view GOP candidates for local office as an extension of the national social conservative movement. This one-size-fits-all view certainly does not help moderate candidates.

At the beginning of 2016, a familiar attack was leveled against New York and New Yorkers. Republican presidential candidate Senator Ted Cruz of Texas attacked fellow candidate Donald J. Trump of New York by saying that he has "New York values." Sure, Trump was being the showman that he is, trolling Cruz by suggesting his Canadian birth made him ineligible to be president of the United States, but Cruz's response only hurt Republicans. He continued to make "New York" a dirty insult.

Talking in this manner only makes it harder for the GOP to build in New York. What sensible New Yorkers would join a party that makes them a punch line? Adding to the problems faced by the local Republican Party of New York is the long history of national Republicans taking stances that negatively impacted New York City. In 1975 New York City was in rough shape when, with hat in hand, New York came to a Republican president—Gerald Ford—to ask for a bailout. Ford responded with a firm "no" and the *New York Daily News* had its iconic headline, "Ford to City: Drop Dead."

What about in 2002 when President George Bush's Office of Management and Budget director, Mitch Daniels, sought to divert over 45 percent of promised post-9/11 reconstruction aid to other programs? A Republican tried to funnel $9 billion away from New Yorkers who had months before suffered the worst terrorist attack in American history.

Only a few months after the worst natural disaster to hit the New York area, Hurricane Sandy, thirty-one Republican senators, including Ted Cruz, voted against providing federal aid for victims. Of course, many of these same senators would later request federal aid for disasters that impacted their own states. This January 2013 vote reeked of hypocrisy.

Then we have the case of H.R.1786[8], the James Zadroga 9/11 Health and Compensation Reauthorization Act that reauthorized the Zadroga Act. Zadroga ensured that the federal government would provide health monitoring and financial assistance to the people who worked in the remnants of the World Trade Center after 9/11. In 2015, Americans watched as national Republicans balked at taking care of New York's Finest and Bravest when the Zadroga Act became permanent. Their rationale? It might cost the United States too much money to take care of our first responders. New Yorkers shook their heads in disbelief. And this wasn't the first time that Republicans said no on this very issue. In 2010, they dragged their heels—while at the same time saying that they would "never forget" the sacrifices made on 9/11—when New Yorkers and Americans united to demand the initial passage of Zadroga. It was the final bill passed in the Democratic-controlled House and brought to the table because Democrats knew that it would not pass when the GOP took the majority in the next session. Only thirty-one House Republicans voted for Zadroga's passage while just one House Democrat voted against it.

Is it really surprising that the decreasing rate of Republicans in New York City, as well as the accompanying increase in New York City Democrats, coincides with these examples of national Republican mistreatment of New Yorkers?

What also did not help Republicans in New York City, as well as other urban areas, was the failure to connect with minority voters, particularly as they became a larger and larger force within the local electorate. The 2010 census found that 33 percent of New Yorkers were white, while African Americans made up 25 percent; 28 percent were Hispanic, and Asians were 13 percent of the population. Republicans did not work to win over minorities on the issues that impacted them and played into the caricature that we are a party for old white men.

In 2013, Joe Lhota, the Republican nominee for mayor of New York City, attempted to change this perception by championing charter schools and the people they benefit. Lhota attended a massive rally and march that saw several thousand minority children and parents walk across the Brooklyn Bridge to New York City Hall and demand that the next mayor treat charter schools fairly. The people who participated in this rally were all part of New York's Democratic base. Yet, to them, they felt like the Democratic Party had abandoned them in favor of the United Federation of Teachers, the powerful teachers union. At first, some were taken aback by a Republican—a member of the party their leaders have castigated for as long as they could remember—joining them. They quickly warmed up to him. (More on this later.)

To these urban minorities, Lhota's interaction was the first direct experience they had had with a Republican in New York. The local Republican Party had largely abandoned their outreach and recruitment. To them, it had little return on investment. With the money saved by not maintaining a presence in Harlem and other solidly Democratic New York neighborhoods, the party could shore up its existing strongholds in places such as Queens and Staten Island, which would make it so they would never be seriously challenged within them. Unfortunately, they failed to take into account the opposition and how they would react. Local Democrats were more than happy for the Republicans to cede future battlegrounds. Now they, too, could save time and money in these areas and divert resources to efforts that allowed them to expand their reach throughout New York City and New York State. All of a sudden, these Republican strongholds, such as Staten Island, became battlegrounds. The party's strategic retreat from prior battlegrounds allowed Democrats to reallocate their own resources and focus on turning the more Republican parts of New York into Democratic ones. Why? Because the local GOP was shortsighted and thought it could save money in the short term.

The long-term consequences of the party's cost-saving moves mean that Republicans have created a self-inflicted wound that hinders them every single election cycle. It is the equivalent of trying to run a marathon the day after running another marathon. Each and every step will be more labored than it should, the exertion more intense, and the ability to fire on all cylinders severely impaired. Reversing this will take an immense amount of time, effort, and money. All of these will cost more than if we had not stopped at all.

The conservative thinker Charles C. W. Cooke noted in his book, *The Conservatarian Manifesto*:

> Over the past half-century, America's progressives have managed successfully to export to the general public a perverted conception of morality in which forever advocating short-term gain at the expel of long-term solvency is somehow a sign of "compassion" and in which reality is expected to bend to meet good intentions and glib slogans and never to break in consequence.[9]

Yes, urban Democrats have sacrificed the fiscal health of the government from the local to the federal levels. They routinely promise exorbitant and wasteful programs and spending priorities to each and every constituency they require in order to ensure they retain the reins of power. These are little more than bribes—which in fairness, Republicans are also guilty of doling out to their own target blocs—that occur every single day within the political world. What sets these apart from their Republican counterparts is their sheer size and scope. As Byron York noted in 2010, of the top fifty senators who used earmarks, thirty-eight were Democrats. Yes, Democrats are incredibly guilty of earmark spending and it is something that the taxpayer cannot afford in the long run.[10]

Let's put this in another, far simpler light. If you are a parent during the holiday season and you want to get gifts for your three children, of course you are going to get them each something that would make them happy beyond words. After all, you want to see them happy and to earn that world's greatest parent title. They each want something that the other two kids will never have an interest in making use of, yet making their dreams come true is what you want to do. You buy your eldest son Jack an action figure that is pretty cool, at least in your book, because of its kung fu grip. Lisa, your daughter, is the apple of your eye, so you buy her a dream house for her dolls. Lastly, your youngest child Robert wants nothing more than the latest gaming system. Of course, you get it for him. You don't have the cash on hand to pay for all of these things, so you put them on a credit card because you will worry about actually paying for these things later. What matters are the smiles on your kids' faces.

After a month of forgetting about paying for the gifts, your credit card bill arrives and demands payment for the toys. This is the moment you realize that you have a problem. In addition to paying for these toys, you also have other pre-existing responsibilities to pay for, such as housing, clothes, food, cable, electricity, and so on and so forth. Given your modest salary, you can't possibly afford to pay for all of these. Your economic situation is now worse because you promised and delivered unique items to each of your children. Now, in order to pay for these obscure luxuries, you will need to borrow more money to pay your bills. When those loans are due to be paid, you will more than likely have to take out new loans again. You are trapped in a vicious cycle.

Republicans, on the other hand, believe at their core that government has a duty to be fiscally responsible. They abhor government waste and believe that the government should only pay for what it truly needs. As a result of this tenet of the party, Republican candidates often campaign for office by touting their fiscal responsibility. They don't stand up and promise the voting public anything and everything. To do so would violate core party doctrine. Sticking to this precept has not helped Republican candidates in the short term, as voters are left to choose between the Democrat promising them a bunch of free and fantastic stuff, and the Republican saying they won't increase spending. In this situation, the Democrat is far more appealing to those who don't consider the long-term implications—unfortunately for both Republicans and Americans in general, voters have repeatedly demonstrated a proclivity to choose short-term gain at long-term expense.

There is the joke that a New York Republican is not a real Republican, but really just a moderate Democrat. It is somewhat insulting, as there is the underlying insinuation that just because we do not adhere to the more socially conservative views of some in the GOP, New York Republicans somehow do not believe in conservatism. The reality is that we believe in conservative ideals and principles. When it comes to social issues, New York Republicans take a hands-off approach. Many can be pro-life and against marriage equality personally, but they do not believe that the government has the right to dictate how a citizen is to live their lives. As a result, many believe New York Republicans to be socially liberal and hold more economically conservative ideals. Furthermore, they believe in a smaller, more limited government, as cities and urban areas are a prime example of the perils of a large and overreaching government. Of course, this should make for the perfect conditions for Republicans to win over new ranks. Alas, due to the aforementioned capitulation and concession of battleground urban areas in cities such as New York, we are unable to take advantage of these conditions. Again, this is not cause for Republicans to throw up their hands and give up on traditionally Democratic-leaning urban areas, but should ignite a burning desire to first make this a true battleground and, ultimately, a Republican-leaning area.

Look at Chicago. It is now plagued with violence, educational failure, and a looming debt crisis—there is also an argument to be made that their "pizza" is also a disaster. Shootings in this city are so bad that many citizens call it "Chiraq." The City of Chicago has a whopping $63.2 billion in debt obligations due to the costs of health care, government pensions, and other debt.[11] This is $23,000 in debt for every Chicago resident. What person wants to be on the hook for such an astronomical sum?!

What is the response of Chicago's elected officials that are Democrats? Raise taxes and don't decrease spending. Another example of the kick-the-can-down-the-road economic approach of Democrats.

In 2014, a venture capitalist launched a bid for governor of Illinois on the Republican Party line. Bruce Rauner and his campaign decided to take advantage of Illinois's primary rules that allow a registered voter to change their party allegiance at the polls. He pushed the issue of unfunded debt, particularly that of unions. With $63.2 billion owed and each resident responsible for $23,000 of it, the fiscal irresponsibility of Democrats and those who sided with the labor unions no matter the cost to the taxpayer was front and center. Fiscally responsible Democrats crossed over and voted for Rauner in the GOP primary. At the same time, the

Chicago's official debt totals $63.2 billion*

All debt and obligations in billions	Pensions	Long-term debt	Retiree health insurance	Total debt	Total debt and obligations per capita
City of Chicago					
City of Chicago	-	$12.0*	$0.5	$12.4	$4,600
Fireman's Annuity and Benefit Fund	$3.0	-	$0.05	$3.1	$1,100
Chicago Police Pension Fund	$6.9	-	$0.2	$7.1	$2,600
Municipal Employees' Annuity and Benefit Fund	$8.4	-	$0.2	$8.6	$3,200
Laborers Pension and Welfare Funds	$1.0	-	$0.04	$1.1	$400
Subtotal	$19.4	$12.0	$0.9	$32.2	$11,900
City of Chicago's sister governments					
Chicago Public Schools	$8.0	$5.6	$3.1	$16.7	$6,200
Chicago Transit Authority (pro-rata)	$0.8	$4.0	-$0.06	$4.8	$1,800
Chicago Park District	$0.4	$0.9	$0.04	$1.4	$500
Subtotal	$9.2	$10.6	$3.1	$22.9	$8,400
Chicago's pro-rata share of Cook County governments					
MWRD	$0.6	$1.4	$0.2	$2.1	$800
Cook County and Forest Preserve	$3.0	$2.1	$1.0	$6.0	$2,200
Subtotal	$3.5	$3.5	$1.2	$8.1	$3,000
Total debt and obligation burden for Chicago taxpayers	$32.1	$26.1	$5.2	$63.2	$23,300

Source: *City of Chicago; Chicago Public Schools; Chicago Transit Authority; Chicago Park District; Cook County; Cook County Forest Preserve; Civic Federation; Metropolitan Water Reclamation District; all associated pension funds; U.S. Census Bureau; Commission on Government Forecasting and Accountability.*

****Note:*** *2012 data used where possible, most recent data available used otherwise. Numbers may not add due to rounding. City of Chicago long-term debt excludes O'Hare and Midway bonds. Long-term debt from all governments is from 2011, with the exception of the city of Chicago, which is from 2012. See Sources and Methodology for more information.*

number of Democratic primary voters fell, which was proof of the Democratic crossover.

The general election proved a bigger challenge than a GOP primary. Illinois is a blue state and statewide Republican candidates face an uphill battle there, too. Forty percent of the state's residents lived in Cook County, which made it the most populous county in Illinois and the second-most populous county in the United States. Solidly Democratic Chicago sat right in the heart of the county. The Rauner campaign set out to nullify that Democratic advantage and attain the goal of securing 43 percent or more in the Cook County suburbs and 20 percent or more of the vote in Chicago.

Rauner pushed conservative themes and issues that held appeal to millennials and urban voters. He addressed the high levels of corruption among elected officials by proposing that lawmakers be subject to term limits. He recognized the problem that the unfunded pensions and massive debt posed, and pushed government spending and pension reform. Addressing the extremely cumbersome bureaucracy that plagued the state, Rauner adopted pro-enterprise and pro-growth tones and policies. Each and every one of these issues and proposals had crossover appeal for Democratic voters. The only question was whether or not it was enough to help Rauner defeat the incumbent Governor Pat Quinn. Would he meet his own benchmarks in Chicago and the Cook County suburbs? Meeting those benchmarks would ensure a victory in the general election.

Part of the strategy for getting these issues into the minds of the voters was to use digital media. Rauner's campaign, which had asked the political consulting firm Bask to oversee its digital operations, used technology to reach the voters when they were online, such as when utilizing the music streaming service Pandora, which ran Rauner campaign ads.

The answer to the question came on November 4, 2014. Governor Quinn secured 46.35 percent of the vote, but Bruce Rauner was able to win with 50.27 percent. In the Cook County suburbs, where he had set the goal of 43 percent of the vote, Rauner received 45.6 percent of that vote. His 20.8 percent achievement in Chicago exceeded his other set goal of 20 percent for that region. In short, the focus on the urban and suburban parts of Cook County paved the way for his impressive win.

Los Angeles is another city with a major Democratic Party advantage. The last time it had a Republican mayor was in 2001, when Richard Riordan served as mayor. Currently, only one Republican, Mitchell Englander, is a member of the fifteen-seat Los Angeles City Council. The other fourteen? All Democrats. Englander is quite literally the minority leader, minority whip, and entire minority conference in the Los Angeles City Council.

According to data found in the Los Angeles Almanac from 2012, over 51 percent of the registered voters in Los Angeles County are registered as Democrats. At the same time, registered Republicans are 21.79 percent of registered voters. That's a lot of Democrats and very few Republicans.

The last time a Republican was mayor of Denver, Colorado?—1963. Like New York City, Denver has not been a prime target—or a target at all—of the Republican Party. Yet, when you look at the politics of Denver residents, there certainly is an argument to be made for Republicans to push socially liberal and fiscally conservative ideas. Let's not forget that Denver led the way in the push to legalize personal consumption and possession of marijuana. In 2005, the City of Denver was the first major city in the United States to enact a law that legalized the possession of an ounce or less of marijuana. The local Republican Party, to what extent there is one, opposed the measure. Denver voters joined Colorado residents in 2012 and made the commercial sale of marijuana legal throughout the state. By a percentage of 55.32 to 44.68, Colorado voters approved Colorado Amendment 64, which amended the state's constitution to allow for personal and commercial use of marijuana. State Republicans chose not to take the opportunity to grow the party by championing the amendment, but rather opposed it. They could have pushed the positive economic impact that the passage of this initiative would have, but they didn't—another instance of a state GOP hurting itself.

The conservative former Colorado congressman and 2010 gubernatorial candidate Tom Tancredo came out in favor of marijuana legalization. He noted that his support for legalization was due to his conservative principles.

> Our nation is spending tens of billions of dollars annually in an attempt to prohibit adults from using a substance objectively less harmful than alcohol.
>
> Yet marijuana is still widely available in our society. We are not preventing its use; we are merely ensuring that all of the profits from the sale of marijuana (outside the medical marijuana system) flow to the criminal underground.[12]

When it comes to big cities and urban areas, Republicans are now rarely elected to the position of mayor or any seat that holds real authority. New York City did elect Rudy Giuliani and Michael Bloomberg, both Republicans, to serve as mayor of New York over five straight elections.

What's the next big city to have a Republican mayor? Not Houston. Not Dallas. Not Chicago. Not Boston. Not Los Angeles. Not Seattle. Not San Francisco. Not Detroit. Not Minneapolis. Not St. Louis. Not Cleveland. Not Philadelphia. Not Baltimore. They are Miami and San Diego. All of these cities listed above that do not have a Republican mayor are thoroughly dominated by Democrats at all levels of government. These cities hold a lot of voters that now are voting Democratic reliably in elections because no GOP presence is in these cities.

Look at the electoral map for a presidential election. The Democratic Party starts each presidential race with over two-hundred electoral votes from seventeen states. In contrast, the Republican

Party begins the race with just over 150 electoral votes from twenty states. The Democratic advantage is solely because of their party's monopoly on urban areas. The three biggest (in terms of electoral votes) reliably Democratic states, California, Illinois, and New York, give Democrats 104 (or 38.5 percent) of the 270 electoral votes required to secure the presidency. Whereas, of the reliably Republican states, we would require a minimum of eight states, which includes Texas and its thirty-eight electoral votes, to achieve that same number. Another important difference to note: Democrats have publicly stated that their goal is to make Texas a purple and ultimately a blue state. Republicans have failed even to make it a goal to win back California, Illinois, and New York. It isn't just alarming; it's a sign that Republicans are not geared toward the future.

It is possible to go from American city to American city and see that over the past few decades, the local governments have moved toward Democratic control and dominance. During this same period, Republicans have willfully abandoned these areas in favor of saving resources for rural and suburban strongholds. This bunker mentality is not a long-term strategy to win elections.

A January 2016 Quinnipiac poll about New York City and its mayor revealed something that should alarm Republicans. This revelation, however, did not come from the polling results, but rather from the polling questions:

- If the election for Mayor were being held today, and the candidates were Bill de Blasio the Democrat, and Scott Stringer running as an independent candidate, for whom would you vote?
- If the election for Mayor were being held today, and the candidates were Bill de Blasio the Democrat, and Ray Kelly running as an independent candidate, for whom would you vote?
- If the election for Mayor were being held today, and the candidates were Bill de Blasio the Democrat, and Ruben

> Diaz Jr. running as an independent candidate, for whom would you vote?[13]

Notice something? All three of these potential challengers to de Blasio would be running as independents and not Republicans. So damaged and decimated is the Republican brand in New York City that running for office citywide as a Republican is unthinkable for any credible candidate. Yes, Quinnipiac changing its own questions to exclude the GOP label does not mean that others will follow suit. What it does portend is how badly the Republican Party is considered and viewed in New York City since Bloomberg was last on the ballot in 2009.

Republicans face a real and looming threat to our survival as a majority party. Our voting base, the baby boomer generation, is shrinking. The popularity of Republicans in urban areas is also diminishing and, in some cases such as New York City, practically nonexistent. Today, the Republican Party faces a choice: stay as it is and see its hold on government dwindle, or adapt and evolve in order to ensure at least thirty more years as the dominant party in American politics. To do the latter, the Republican Party must turn toward millennials.

Older strategists and voters are hesitant to embrace millennials. If you merely mention millennials, their eyes glaze over and they tune out. Their knee-jerk reaction is one of dismissal. When they hear the word millennial, the consultants and voters picture young college kids that are smoking pot in their parents' basement, not registered to vote, very liberal, not politically active (or backing Bernie Sanders because it is "cool"), and have no concept of pressing issues. It's a false and incorrect assumption.

When it comes to millennials, we need to act—and fast. Millennials, men and women who are aged eighteen through thirty-four, are the largest voting bloc in the United States. Additionally, in 2015, they overtook baby boomers as the biggest generation in the country, numbering a whopping 75.3 million people. They are the biggest portion of the US labor force. With over 23 percent of Americans being a member of the millennial generation, their voices will be heard at the voting booth and this shall happen for decades to come.

The assumption of the older Republican consultants, operatives, and voters about millennials is way off. The reality is that millennials are not the pothead college students that they are made out to be. Older millennials now have families of their own

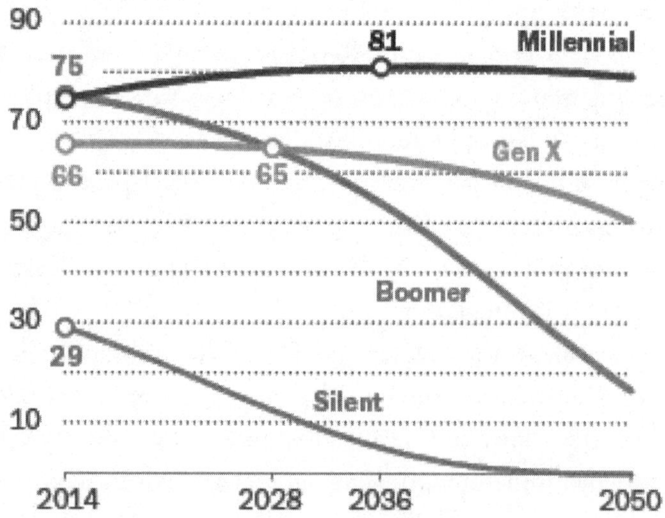

Millennials are Americans born between 1982 and 1994. Baby boomers are people born between 1946 and 1964. Silent generation members were born between 1925 and 1945. Gen X members were born between 1966 and 1976.

and are incredibly concerned about and engaged in the issues that confront us. They care about education. They care about entitlements. They care about health care. They care about national security. They care about immigration. They care about marriage equality. They care about what is going on and where we as a nation are headed.

In the United States, the interests of millennials are ones that are tailor-made for conversion to the Republican Party. They are a diverse group of men and women who are socially more libertarian and economically more conservative. One in four Americans between the ages of twenty-five and thirty-four, which is part of the age range that qualifies one for being a millennial, live in a multigenerational home. This number has more than doubled since 1980. They have also overtaken the oldest Americans who were most likely to live in a multigenerational home. The reason for this? The cost of living has increased drastically. So these Americans make the conscious choice to live at home in order to save money for the future.

The Pew Research Center notes that this trend toward multigenerational homes has not only happened to millennials, but to other generations, not to mention all races and ethnicities.

> The increase in multigenerational living since 2010 is apparent across genders and among most racial and ethnic groups. While the share of young adults ages 25 to 34 living in multigenerational households has increased most rapidly, the share increased across all age groups with one exception: Among those ages 65 to 84, the share living in a multigenerational household decreased slightly between 2010 and 2012.[14]

What has caused this to happen? For one, affordability and cost of living have become prevalent issues that impact the daily lives of Americans. The Great Recession of 2008 put the economy front and center in the minds of Americans as the world seemed to have an economic meltdown. Abstract economic concepts that most people had barely ever heard of or understood had caused the worst financial crisis since the Great Depression. The very real consequences were felt by all and the worry it caused around the family dinner table was palpable.

In the United States, the Great Recession caused 8.7 million jobs to be lost, the unemployment rate to rise from 4.7 percent to over 10 percent, and the gross domestic product (GDP) to contract by 5.1 percent. The United States came to the brink of economic collapse and was able to rescue itself. This economic disaster was felt by all Americans, and for millennials, it was their first real experience with real world economics. The Great Recession helped to shape the views of millennials on what they believed to be right and wrong when it came to economic policy.

Singular and startling events, like the Great Recession, can drastically alter the views of society, particularly the generation that comes of age when it occurs. Pearl Harbor immediately changed the mindset of the United States public from one that was prone toward isolationism to a more intervention-minded belief system. Prior to December 7, 1941, members of the silent generation, who would ultimately become the parents of baby boomers, were accustomed to feeling safe and secure from the regional conflicts that were erupting in the rest of the world. Japanese and German aggression in the world was not the problem of the United States. In fact, a small but notable minority of Americans publicly supported the actions of Adolf Hitler and Germany. Overnight, this changed as the United States entered the Second World War.

The terrorist attacks of September 11, 2001, were also such a moment. The shock, horror, and scope of the tragedy all introduced to older millennials the real dangers of the world in which we live. Instantly, it imprinted itself on the psyche of these first millennials; 9/11 was an important part of the formulation of their view of the world. They recognized that the threats they faced were far different than those faced by prior generations. Invading armies are now about as threatening to the United States as Canada becoming the American football capital of the world.

However, millennials today are more resistant to engage in preemptive action because of how the War in Iraq unfolded. The vast majority of the United States supported President George W. Bush's decision to invade Afghanistan after the 9/11 attacks, as it was a fairly black and white issue. Despite overwhelming initial support of invasion, the country was more divided by Bush's belief that in order to stabilize the Middle East, the threat of Saddam Hussein's Iraq had to be eliminated. Liberal Democrats opposed it from the outset, with many taking to the streets to protest against such an invasion. Once Iraq descended into chaos, the country split over ideological lines, as we wound up in a guerilla war that lasted for years. Capitalizing on the fatigue generated by almost a decade of war, Barack Obama removed the United States presence from Iraq, which ultimately helped to create the threat of ISIS.

Unfortunately, Republicans are suffering from the backlash of Obama's actions, as the left and the media are blaming Bush for the current situation confronting our country. To millennials and urban voters, the Republican Party is too militant, and its policies create future enemies. In actuality, Bush's invasion of Iraq was the right thing to do, despite several problems that could have been avoided in the post-invasion management of Iraq. It removed a despotic dictator who engaged in gross human rights abuses and genocide. The world is a better place without him in power. Sure, in 2016 the whole idea is less popular among Republicans than it was in the Bush years, but why is that? Americans are justifiably tired of war, which certainly is a contributing factor to the decreased support for the Iraq War today. However, that frustration with war and how post-war Iraq turned is more a result of President Obama's leadership than that of President Bush. It was Obama whose actions created the global chaos we see today. Russia is emboldened, ISIS is spreading across the world, and American influence has declined. Had we stayed the course and followed Bush's plan through, it is a fair bet that many of the issues we face today would not have occurred.

When Bush increased the number of American troops in Iraq to stabilize a disintegrating situation in 2007, Iraq was put back on course to stability and security. It was President Obama's premature withdrawal of American forces that was completed in 2011 that turned out to be the problem. Experts point to how this action by Obama caused the problems that the world faces today. However, to hear Obama say it, the withdrawal and its consequences are the fault of his predecessor, George W. Bush. The accusation would be laughable if it weren't reflective of an administration more interested in winning a public relations war more than an actual war.

Over 80 percent of the United States population lives in an urban area, according to the 2010 United States Census.[15] This includes suburban areas as well. That is over 245 million Americans. Most urban residents do not connect with the Republican Party and its candidates. Think about that.

Rural voters are already solidly in the Republican tent. The GOP has them so locked up that Democrats have decided to give up even trying to get these voters to vote for their candidates. They won't be turning out in the general election for the Democratic Party and its candidates, but Democrats do try to get them to not vote at all. They know that if rural voters don't cast their vote, Republicans are going to have a hard time winning an important election, as the GOP is all about turning out its base. Democrats seek to suppress the vote by engaging in deceitful tactics that seek to cut the ties the base has with the Republican candidate. They seek to embarrass and destroy the image of the candidate, with the goal of making them unpalatable. They find any bit of information about a candidate that they can and then spin it. The most famous instance of this is the 2000 presidential election when it was revealed the George W. Bush had plead guilty to driving under the influence in 1976. The story was released to Fox News by Chris Lehane, a Democratic operative for Al Gore's presidential campaign. The timing of the release of the youthful indiscretion was designed to paint Bush as lacking in moral fiber and cause many social conservatives to stay home on Election Day. Many believe that were it not for this, Bush would have won the election outright and Florida's recount would have not happened.

So much for the Democratic Party's claim that they are playing to the better angels of the American voters.

The midterm elections of 2014 should offer hope to Republicans. Not only did we retake the majority in the United States Senate, but something noteworthy happened; turnout among urban voters dropped 47 percent.[16] This clearly showed that urban voters were not buying what Democrats were selling. At the same time, it demonstrated that urban voters were not exactly going to be buying what we Republicans were selling either. Instead, they were opting to sit out elections entirely. This might be viewing this statistic as "glass half full," but it shows that the hold Democrats have on urban voters is far more fragile than many believe it to be.

President Obama has a gift. He's a talented and inspirational speaker. His ability to communicate is one that many politicians would love to have. Of course, when it comes to Iraq, he put this skill to use, exploited national dissatisfaction with the overall Iraq War, and shifted the blame to Bush. This is an example of how the Republican Party has had an issue connecting to the American public, especially since we are currently lacking a star that can communicate like Obama, Bill Clinton, or Ronald Reagan. Further, the GOP has had some issues with its overall message, as it does not appeal to millennials and urban voters. It actually turns them off and makes us look like we belong in the past. (Of course, Donald Trump's presidential campaign further cemented this view.) This creates yet another hurdle that we, as a party, must overcome.

Millennials are primed to be members of the Republican Party, but we need to work to get them there. We need to change how we talk to them and adopt new methods of speaking to voters. On top of this, we have to present our conservative views and values in a manner that is palatable to millennials and urban residents. This does not mean just putting a spin on the long-held beliefs of the party. What must be done requires that the party adapt and evolve its views to the world as it is today. Voters are changing the way they view the issues, so why isn't the Republican Party?

As issues such as equality, social justice, and paid family leave arise, Republicans are reflexively opposing them because they are being put forth by Democrats (it is also fair to note that Democrats oppose GOP issues because they are proposed by Republicans). It is the culture of political warfare in which we live. Knifing your political opponent can be a lot of fun, but it isn't always going to help the end goal of achieving party growth. To be clear, there are times in political undertakings where more divisive tactics are warranted, but they should only be used after careful deliberation on the best course of action to take in order to achieve your goal. We need not be a nation with a multitude of wannabe Frank Underwoods leading us.

What should be done is a thorough evaluation of Democratic proposals and issues that could be used by Republicans to advance our goals and ideas. When push comes to shove, Republicans are not always right and Democrats are not always wrong. There is room on many of the issues Democrats are pushing on social justice and equality that are in the heart of conservatism. Republicans have a different approach to these issues than Democrats and this approach is one that is beneficial to Americans.

In 2014, there was a golden opportunity for Republicans to divide and conquer the New York City electorate. Progressive Democrats had proposed the creation of a new tax for the use of plastic bags at stores. It would require stores to charge New Yorkers ten cents per bag, be it paper or plastic, that the store provided for the purchased goods. The tax was designed to encourage consumers to bring their own reusable bags to the store to place their groceries in. One proponent, City Councilman Brad Lander (D-Brooklyn) called the tax an "incentive"—hello, Big Government—to change people's behavior.

This "Plastic Bag Tax" as it was known, disproportionately impacted and targeted poor urban minorities—the very segment of the population that urban Democrats claim to represent. Republicans chose not to take advantage of this opening provided by the progressive Democrats. Instead, they chose to save money and resources by letting the moderate Democrats serve as the opposition. This is part of the pattern of the Republican Party surrendering the fight in urban areas.

Were this fight to happen again today, Republicans should go all in and use this as a way to alienate urban voters from the Democratic Party. First, we would employ a public relations campaign that painted all Democrats as being in support of a policy that "taxes people for being poor." Extreme characterization? Sure, but this is a fight that we are in, and these tactics are certainly warranted. The argument is whether to make citizens pay for not behaving in a manner that the progressive segment of the population believes you should behave in, or you follow their rigid rules and ideologies. It is essentially a fine or tax to live your life differently.

The next step is to work on public outreach. Republicans should quietly work with other opponents of the measure to organize rallies and other events that were established in opposition. During the course of these meetings and happenings, operatives should be actively acquiring the emails and phone numbers of the participants. With these, we could build lists for future use in campaigns and party undertakings. If we can get opponents of the Plastic Bag Tax to agree with us on this issue, then we can certainly persuade them to agree with us Republicans on other issues.

Finally, we could use the results of this in challenging the supporters of the Plastic Bag Tax when they are up for reelection or when they attempt to run for higher office. Their stance is part of their own record and we can use this against them when the time comes to defeat them at the ballot box. It's a model that can be replicated over and over again.

Employing these tactics should not be viewed either by the public or the Republican Party as an attempt to depress turnout in an election. Shrinking voter turnout in an election in order for your side to win might work, but it is not a long-term solution to the problems confronting the GOP in urban areas. We can and must use messaging to argue why the Democratic agenda is not advantageous to urban voters and millennials, but we must also offer a viable alternative.

Having been left unchecked in their urban growth, the Democratic Party and its elected officials have not had the reality check of a true opposition party. Since Republican-elected officials are scarce to nonexistent in urban areas, Democrats have had a free-for-all in progressive legislation that is harmful to the city in which it is enacted. The Plastic Bag Tax, which was voted into law by the New York City Council in the spring of 2016, is just one example of how we can use the proposals of Democrats against them.

Democrats are quite literally giving Republicans great ammunition to use against them. They have gone so long without being held accountable by a true opposition party and its candidates, that there is little fear of repercussion at the ballot box if they veer too far to the left and the extreme. Their policies on almost every single issue are wrong and detrimental to urban residents and millennials. Any potential Republican candidate for office should be ecstatic about these facts. However, they face the problem of the local Republican Party apparatus.

The party's conscious decision to pull out of battleground precincts in urban areas and focus on shifting resources to strongholds (several of which later became battlegrounds) weakened the ability of future candidates to launch a successful campaign for office. GOP candidates have a tough race to run, as they not only are going to have to start their race with little to no preexisting infrastructure, but they have to work to combat the view that they are the caricature the left and media have made them out to be.

Chapter 3

Hello, I would like to add you to my social network

EVERY SINGLE MORNING, I WAKE UP, ROLL OVER, PET MY DOG, and reach for my iPhone. First, I browse through the multitude of emails I received since I went to sleep five hours earlier. I read the morning email news roundups from *Politico*, *Politico New York*, and other news outlets. After firing off quick replies to emails that can't wait, I open my Twitter app and find out what the dominant stories and conversations of the morning are. I post a few tweets and then switch over to Facebook to see what the talk of that digital town is. I then check my email and Twitter again. It is a routine that lasts anywhere from thirty minutes to an hour. Once out of bed, I am glued to my phone, even when there are competing interests. I might be working or watching TV, but I still check my phone every couple of minutes. My day ends and night begins, and all the while my iPhone gets a decent amount of use. This happens right through when I go to bed. It isn't just seeing what's happening in the world, but getting to see the picture of the cat that looks pissed off or some really delicious looking dish that a friend is eating.

This routine is something common to most millennials. We are constantly plugged in and engaged with what is happening online. Our digital addiction is one that makes us feel part of a larger community, where we share experiences with one another. It doesn't matter if the experience is a serious one such as a natural disaster like Hurricane Sandy, or a funny one like debating whether a dress is blue and black, or white and gold. What does matter is that we are all experiencing the event, no matter how trivial, together. Suddenly, such a big world is incredibly small and intimate.

Coinciding with the rise of millennials has been the emergence of social media and networking platforms. Facebook, Twitter, Instagram, Snapchat . . . the list of social platforms that have come to dominate American and global culture goes on and on. As a result of social media, we live in a constantly connected world, where millennials in particular are constantly posting, sharing, liking, and viewing their own narrative, as well as the narratives of their friends.

Not only are millennials interacting with their friends and family on social media, but they are interacting with brands. Why shouldn't they be engaged with their political candidates, parties, and beliefs? The truth is that they are and seek to be.

Both the Republican and Democratic parties have built sophisticated social media outreach operations designed to get voters to volunteer, contribute and, ultimately, vote for their candidates in elections. However, because it is still a relatively new arena in the political world, candidates for office are less likely to embrace or build the social media operations that are needed for communicating with millennials. There is little investment by the majority of campaigns in the digital realm. These candidates might as well be fighting with one hand tied behind their back.

The truth of the matter is that the smaller the election or issue campaign, the less likely it is to utilize social media to win support and votes. The reason for this is that resources on any sort of campaign are scarce and each area of the campaign is competing against all others for its share of the pie. Throw in the demand for paid advertising and direct mail, which quite often involves consultants and operatives taking a few "percentage points" of the buy—in addition to their regular fee—and there is a large money suck. Many of these same consultants and operatives relegate social media components and the aides tasked with overseeing them to the status of outcast and window dressing. They view social and digital as a peculiar and mostly alien field that has yet to prove itself. Some even mistakenly believe that the people who use social media are some sort of nerds that lack social skills and rarely leave their mom's basement. Of course, this perception is false.

The use of social media among Americans has increased nine times over from 2005 through 2015. It is expected to keep growing. Most adults in the United States have at least one social media account, be it Instagram, Facebook, Twitter, Snapchat, or some other network. In 2005, 7 percent of Americans used social media. By the end of 2015, the number was 65 percent. That's 22.3 million Americans in 2005 growing to 207.3 million Americans in 2015—an astronomical rate of growth. Still, a full 111.7 million people, 35 percent of the populace, are out there, waiting to connect with us on digital platforms.

Millennials procure their news from "non-traditional" resources. They do not buy a daily newspaper, turn on their nightly news, or browse the latest magazines. Instead, they seek to learn about the world and its events through the mediums that they are comfortable with: social media.

A full 61 percent of millennials use Facebook to get their daily news, while only 37 percent use television as their source of information. Baby boomers, on the other hand, are the polar opposite of millennials and news gathering. Thirty-nine percent acquire their news from Facebook and 60 percent use local television.

Millennials and Baby Boomers: A Generational Divide in Sources Relied on for Political News

% who got news about politics and government in the previous week from...

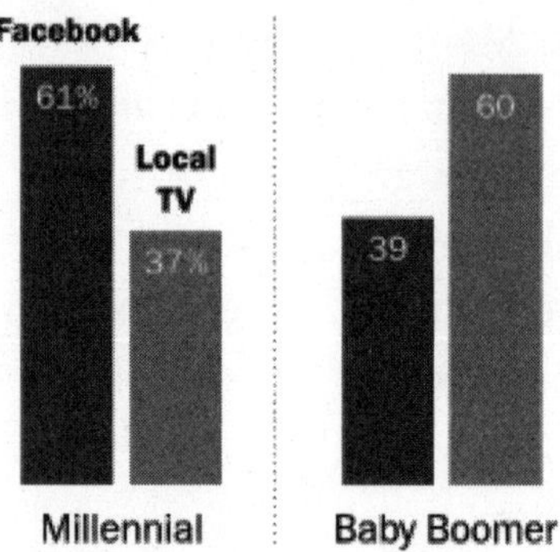

American Trends Panel (wave 1). Survey conducted March 19-April 29, 2014. Q22, Q24A. Based on online adults.

PEW RESEARCH CENTER

What other breakdowns are there in social media usage among Americans? Pew found the following:

- **Age differences: Seniors make strides**. Young adults (ages eighteen to twenty-nine) are the most likely to use social media—fully 90 percent do. Still, usage among those sixty-five and older has more than tripled since 2010 when 11 percent used social media. Today, 35 percent of all those sixty-five and older report using social media, compared with just 2 percent in 2005.
- **Gender differences: Women and men use social media at similar rates.** Women were more likely than men to use social networking sites for a number of years, although since 2014 these differences have been modest. Today, 68 percent of all women use social media, compared with 62 percent of all men.
- **Socioeconomic differences: Those with higher education levels and household income lead the way.** Over the past decade, it has consistently been the case that those in higher-income

households were more likely to use social media. More than half (56 percent) of those living in the lowest-income households now use social media, though growth has leveled off in the past few years. Turning to educational attainment, a similar pattern is observed. Those with at least some college experience have been consistently more likely than those with a high school degree or less to use social media over the past decade. The first year that more than half of those with a high school diploma or less used social media was in 2013.

- **Racial and ethnic similarities:** There are not notable differences by racial or ethnic group: 65 percent of whites, 65 percent of Hispanics, and 56 percent of African Americans use social media today.
- **Community differences: More than half of rural residents now use social media.** Those who live in rural areas are less likely than those in suburban and urban communities to use social media, a pattern consistent over the past decade. Today, 58 percent of rural residents, 68 percent of suburban residents, and 64 percent of urban residents use social media.

Given the trends and tendencies of millennials, it is important that political parties, campaigns, and candidates learn about the changing landscape and adapt. This is true at every level, be it a presidential or local assembly race. Part of this adaptation is recognizing that social media has a vital role to play in the campaigns of today. It is how we millennials consume all of our news and learn about what is going on in the world. Yet still, campaigns are not fully immersed and invested in the digital world.

The trepidation among the old guard is real, despite the proof of the value of a strong digital presence. In 2012, Barack Obama's reelection campaign stunned everyone by utterly dominating the digital portion of the election. Not only was his campaign actively communicating with voters on social media, they were wisely using digital analytics and modeling to see what messages resonated with voters, how turnout could be improved, and how the campaign could be made more cost-effective. It was and is the gold standard of presidential campaigns in terms of its use of digital.

During each campaign cycle, we see one or two candidates emerge as the candidate(s) of change and innovation. This change and innovation are not in terms of their message, but in how they revolutionize the digital realm to outperform their opponents. Sometimes, as in the case of Howard Dean in 2004, they do not win their race, but it is not the fault of their digital operation. In Dean's campaign, his digital team found three new ways to connect and engage voters. First, he utilized the social networking site Meetup in order to organize his followers, both formally and informally. Dean supporters could now find one another locally and help with a grassroots campaign. Additionally, his campaign made use of blogs to get his message out. Finally, he began using online fund-raising appeals that made use of news events in real time. When news broke, the Dean campaign would send out a fund-raising email, using it as a specific reason to give money to support the candidate.

Dean failed in his bid for the Democratic nomination, but his campaign advanced the digital game for all. In the general election, another presidential campaign took the ball of digital progress and ran with it. George W. Bush's reelection campaign (it should be noted that George Bush's 2000 presidential campaign also used this) made use of a retail marketing tool that had not previously been used in the political arena: microtargeting.

Microtargeting was best summarized by *The New York Times*:

> Microtargeting uses computers and mathematical models to take disparate bits of information about voters—the cars they own, the groups they belong to, the magazines they read—and analyze it in a way to predict how likely a person is to vote and what issues and values are most important to him.[17]

Bush's campaign was able to use the predictive models on voter behavior to pinpoint the beliefs of voters and use them to refine their campaign message. Microtargeting also encouraged the Bush campaign to not expend energy and resources trying to convince voters that would never come around to their candidate. Bush's opponent, then Senator John Kerry of Massachusetts, and his campaign felt confident on Election Day 2004. Many within the Kerry campaign felt that their message and opposition to Bush and his policies were enough to get them to 270 electoral votes. As polls began to close, some of Kerry's top aides were rumored to have begun calling him, "Mr. President." Bush's reelection stunned them and Kerry conceded the race the next day.

Smart strategists from both sides of the aisle began to study the intricacies of Dean's and Bush's digital games. Even smarter ones adapted the Dean digital playbook, and then evolved it. By the 2008 presidential election, it was a whole new ball game.

"Were it not for the Internet, Barack Obama would not be president. Were it not for the Internet, Barack Obama would not have been the nominee," said Arianna Huffington.[18] She was broadly correct. Huffington should have said were it not for a strong digital operation, Barack Obama would not be president. Were it not for a strong digital operation, Barack Obama would not have been the nominee.

In 2008, then Senator Barack Obama took digital politics to new heights. He and his campaign brain trust decided to think outside the box by hiring the best digital operatives available . . . even if they had never worked in politics. Sure, one could hire the top political digital operatives, but they would be nowhere nearly as proficient as hiring somebody with private sector experience in the social media capital of the world: Silicon Valley. Enter Chris Hughes.

Hughes, a Harvard graduate, knew a thing or two about social media. After all, he was one of the cofounders of Facebook. A complete lack of political experience would scare away most campaign managers from hiring a person for anything but a grunt position. However, the Obama campaign leadership recognized that Hughes and other members of the Silicon Valley community were light-years ahead of the pack when it came to digital and social media. Hughes was hired to help lead Obama's new media apparatus. His Silicon Valley approach to things was evident from the start, as his official title was "Online Organizing Guru." One can almost hear the collective groan let out by the old guard of consultants and operatives when they heard this position name. At the time, the hiring of Chris Hughes was seen as an odd-to-risky move by Obama. In hindsight, it was pure genius.

The first thing the Obama campaign did was to institute a social network of its own, My.BarackObama.com, which allowed supporters to create their own Facebook-like profile on the Obama campaign website. On this profile page, supporters were empowered to create their own fund-raising campaigns, volunteer either in person or digitally, organize locally, write a letter to the editor, and much, much more. What did this get Obama? It helped him raise what was, at the time, a record breaking $600 million. It built a sophisticated list of emails and data on voters.

The Obama campaign embraced a digital-first attitude, which was evident in how it handled announcing its vice presidential selection. With every presidential nominee, the guessing game of who will be on the bottom half of the ticket is an obsession. People of all stripes make their picks as to who would be the best fit for the nominee, but it is purely a parlor game. The only person that it is not a game for is the actual presidential nominee. The press trip over themselves trying to read the tea leaves and decipher what, if any, hints there are that somebody might be picked. Traditionally, a campaign announces its VP pick by leaking it to the media and having an announcement rally soon thereafter. Obama didn't play by those rules. Instead, he cleverly told any and everyone who would listen that the announcement would be made via a mass text message to any and all who wanted to receive it. He was bypassing the filter of the media and talking directly to the American public. What did this cost the people who wanted to receive this message? All they had to do was fill out a form that provided a bit of personal information and they would be the first to know.

The Obama campaign had successfully leveraged a major news event into a way to collect a massive amount of valuable data and information on voters from the actual voters. Even more commendable is that they had convinced these voters to give them this data entirely voluntarily.

The Obama campaign's social network, My.BarackObama.com, went further than the normal practice of allowing campaigns to reach supporters; it made it possible for supporters to reach one another. The other 2008 presidential campaigns might as well have been talking to people by using signal fires.

The technology news site Mashable listed the following (including the accompanying explanations) as major victories and accomplishments of the 2008 Obama campaign:

- **Twitter:** Obama joined Twitter in March 2007, and by Election Day 2008, he was one of the most popular people on the microblog. He had more than 118,000 followers, while his Republican rival McCain had a mere 4,942. The Obama campaign would tweet several times each week. Though now this sounds like a small number, it showed a strong commitment to Twitter in the platform's early days.
- **YouTube:** The Obama campaign used YouTube to spread 14.5 million hours of official video footage—all for free. According to political consultant Joe Trippi, that quantity of visibility on network television would have cost $47 million.
- **MySpace:** Obama had about four times as many friends on MySpace as his competitor McCain (844,927 versus 219,404)—a huge advantage, though not as pronounced as his Twitter lead.
- **My.BarackObama.com:** Jumping on the social networking bandwagon, the campaign created My.BarackObama.com, the

first robust social platform for campaign supporters to engage with others on issues relating to the campaign. After Obama's victory, the campaign decided to keep the platform up and running. The campaign also used Change.gov—the official website—to ask citizens to share their stories and goals.

- **Vice Presidential Text Announcement:** The Obama campaign rewarded supporters by sending them a text message with the announcement of the vice president pick first. The text read, "Barack has chosen Senator Joe Biden to be our VP nominee. Watch the first Obama-Biden rally live at 3pm ET on www.barackobama.com. Spread the word!"[19]

The other campaigns simply had the snot kicked out of them.

Right after Election Day 2008, Republicans knew they had a problem. Not only had Barack Obama been overwhelmingly elected as the forty-fourth president of the United States, his digital campaign was light-years ahead of, well . . . everybody.

Republicans convened meeting after meeting with the goal of leveling the playing field against Obama in 2012. Former Massachusetts Governor Mitt Romney, the Republican nominee in 2012, empowered his campaign to try to beat Obama at his own game. The best GOP digital operatives went out and created ORCA, a sophisticated app that could mobilize and empower the Romney campaign's over thirty thousand operatives, staffers, and volunteers. With ORCA, they would get out the vote and push Romney past the 270 electoral votes he needed to become the forty-fifth president of the United States. On Election Day 2012, the Romney campaign was confident that they would emerge victorious. So confident were Romney and his top advisors, his campaign eschewed tradition and superstition by having only one speech written: a victory speech. Many operatives, no matter what generation they are a part of, believe that a campaign tempts fate by not having both a victory and concession speech prepared.

State after state closed their polls and as each one was called, the mood at the Romney campaign shifted from excited anticipation to disbelief. The exit polls the news networks were using, showing that Obama was wiping the floor with Romney, had to be wrong. ORCA, which the campaign had bet so heavily on, was supposed to be the secret weapon that gave Romney the edge and the Oval Office. Soon, it became readily apparent that Governor Romney needed to write a concession speech.

What the Romney campaign failed to consider was that the day after Barack Obama was elected to the presidency in 2008, his team was already gearing up for 2012. His digital operatives knew that what they did in 2008 would be obsolete by the 2012 election. They immediately set out to use data to recruit the best tech talent that Silicon Valley had to offer. Obama sent emissaries to entreat this talent with a simple sales pitch: come work for President Obama's reelection campaign, abandon a social life to work ungodly hours that might as well be 24/7, and change the world by having free reign to create the most sophisticated digital political operation in history. The sales pitch worked.

Obama 2012 built on Obama 2008 by first keeping his core digital team largely intact. Chris Hughes might have been gone, but the Obama brain trust was in no way hindered. They once again embraced and pioneered the use of big data to improve the way the campaign worked overall. It found efficiencies across the board and helped with voter mobilization.

The areas in which the Obama 2012 campaign was ahead of the curve were numerous. Obama made use of new digital technologies to outperform the Romney campaign on all fronts. First, he enabled supporters to donate to the campaign via text. It was the first presidential campaign to employ this function. Supporters were able to donate up to $50 by texting the word "give" to Obama (62262). It was simple, fast, and convenient. Gone was the requirement that you donate by filling out a bunch of information on a webpage or paper donation form. Obama's team also expanded their ability to receive donations by making use of Square, a mobile payment app that was another platform that simplified donations.

Many social networks emerged during Obama's first term. Instagram, a photo sharing app, became a major social network among millennials. Obama's digital team recognized the importance of Instagram and quickly built a strategy that would help the campaign with voters. The Obama Instagram playbook was brilliant: use the app as a way to provide Americans with exclusive, behind-the-scenes access to the president and Mrs. Obama. Each and every photo that was posted was an inside look into what you don't see on TV. It had the goal of creating a sense of intimacy and a personal relationship between the user and Obama.

My.BarackObama.com was antiquated by the time 2012 rolled around. The Obama campaign adapted and evolved it to function at maximum impact for the reelection effort. This resulted in the new version of My.BarackObama.com, a new personal Obama platform: Dashboard.

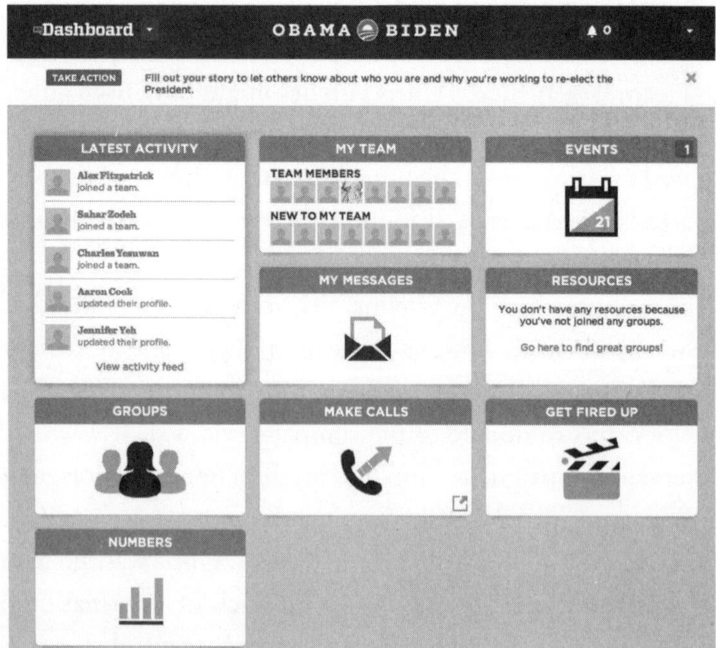

Dashboard was created to be a digital field office for supporters throughout the country. Every single member of this network were now handed the keys to their own digital field office that was able to provide nearly the exact same capabilities of the traditional brick-and-mortar campaign field offices. Dashboard did have one flaw; it was not the most effective tool to use on a mobile device.

In order to compensate for Dashboard's less-than-ideal mobile device capabilities, the Obama campaign created its own mobile app. The app, which was available for iPhone and Android, allowed voters to RSVP for campaign events, donate money to the campaign, receive information on how or where to vote, as well as a host of other information. It was another facet of the overwhelmingly sophisticated Obama digital operation.

The Obama campaign also knew that President Obama's greatest strength was the ability to inspire and provoke an emotional response from people. They sought greater ways for him to connect directly with the voters and his supporters. Not everybody could get out to a campaign rally or speech. What people could do is go online. They could already visit social networking sites and directly interact with the virtual Obama, but what about a more direct interaction facilitated by digital platforms?

Twitter, Facebook, Reddit, and Google Hangouts all presented the opportunity to allow President Obama to engage his supporters through unique question and answer sessions that optimized each social network's inherent strengths. For Twitter, the campaign would schedule Twitter events where the president would answer the questions of his audience. In order to ask a question, all a person had to do was tweet the question with the predetermined hashtag, such as #forward, and the president might tweet his answer to your question. The same idea was employed on Facebook, but with a post asking for questions to be posted in the comments. He did Reddit AMAs (Ask Me Anything), too. Finally, Obama participated in Google Hangouts, which were digital town halls. In order to participate in these, all one needed was a Google account and a computer with a webcam (by this time they were standard issue in most laptops). All of these helped to foster a closer and more intimate connection for the supporter with Obama.

There is a saying that some digital operatives live by. If given a choice between viewing a social media post that is a plan for world peace or viewing a picture of a cat doing something funny, most would choose the cat. Not only would they choose the cat, but they would help it go viral by sharing it with their friends across their social networks. The Obama team recognized that social media is a place where humor is prevalent and key to dominating the conversation.

When Clint Eastwood delivered his address to the Republican National Convention in 2012, he did so with a prop, an empty chair. He used the chair to conduct a mock interview with an imaginary President Obama. It was a bit off and was immediately viewed as a weird stunt. Of course, the press asked Obama and his campaign for their reaction. The Obama campaign's response was brilliant. Instead of having his campaign press office put out a statement in reaction, the Obama digital team posted a picture on Twitter of the president sitting in his chair in a cabinet meeting with a simple quote, "This seat's taken," which was accompanied by a link to his campaign site. The tweet was retweeted over fifty-six thousand times and viewed several million times—that doesn't even count the number of people who saw it because the media did stories on the picture itself (where the picture was featured prominently in these press reports). This was one of countless instances where the Obama campaign used wit and humor to succeed.

After Election Day 2012, once again Republican digital operatives immediately began planning for 2016. The mood was somber, as ORCA was supposed to stop the Goliath that was the Obama digital campaign. The question that was on everybody's mind was *what the hell just happened?*

Unlike the Romney campaign, the Obama campaign chose to fly more under the radar in its digital efforts. Why reveal their hand in the middle of the game? It made no sense to show your opponent your cards until after the election. The Romney campaign on the other hand could not help itself. They were proud of ORCA. Feeling they should celebrate it and also preempt any questions on whether or not they were up to taking on the Obama digital juggernaut, the Romney team began revealing the inner workings of ORCA and its digital operations to the press long before a single vote was cast in the general election. In the short-term, the story was one the Romney campaign liked. The media was running with the narrative

Romney's campaign wanted, that he had caught up to and possibly even surpassed Obama in the digital realm. Obama's response, utter silence, seemed to confirm this notion. After Election Day, it became apparent that nothing could be further from the truth. The Obama campaign had lived by the saying that those who speak don't know and those who know don't speak.

ORCA failed because it was built more for a 2008 presidential campaign and not for 2012. Its architects were not as digitally savvy as Obama's and they wound up building a flawed system. For example, on Election Day, ORCA crashed and left the people it was meant to help flying blind. In fact, there was not even a test run of ORCA conducted to expose any flaws that could hurt Romney on the first Tuesday in November.[20] ORCA was Republicans using minor league tools against a major league team. To quote Rick Perry, "Oops."

Republicans went about their digital autopsy of 2012 and were simply in awe. They set out to not be beaten for a third consecutive presidential election and went all in. Soon the reality set in that digital success in 2016 and beyond would require some heavy lifting. This undertaking will require significant investment, which many within the party see as necessary.

Certainly, some in the Republican Party will look at the cost of outreach to millennials and wonder if the return on investment is really worth it. After all, in the 2014 midterm elections, only 21.3 percent of millennials voted. In the same election, baby boomers voted at nearly twice the rate that millennials did. According to exit polls, 37 percent of people aged sixty and older voted in the 2014 midterms. Why shouldn't we stick to catering to a voting bloc that turns out far more reliably than millennials?

The answer is simple. Baby boomers have far fewer election cycles left in which they can vote, whereas millennials have far more. (We have to be brutally honest with ourselves about this fact.) Actually, this statement should be revised to say that baby boomers can keep pace with millennials and vote in the same election cycles, but after a certain point, they will be party to election fraud, as the dead don't ordinarily vote—although, in 1960, they remarkably rose up as a zombie horde and cast their vote for John F. Kennedy in Chicago.

There already have been whispers among the old guard of Republican operatives and consultants that we should cede the digital ground to the Democrats—just like Republicans did in urban areas. In their view, this would allow the party and its candidates to save money and resources that could be spent on other endeavors. This logic is not only exceedingly stupid, but dangerous to the future of the Republican Party. Giving up the digital game in an era when digital devices dominate our daily lives is the equivalent of giving up on using radio and TV to communicate with voters within the first decade or two of their existence. So connected are Americans to digital experiences, we have had to update our laws and public service announcements to increase public safety. Texting while driving is illegal in most states. Cities tell their citizens to not use their smartphones when crossing the street. Movie theaters tell patrons to silence and not use their mobile devices during films—actually, Congress should consider instating the death penalty for any and all who violate this sacred commandment. The list of new digital device manners and laws is endless.

Part of moving toward a more millennial-facing strategy in the Republican Party is to communicate with them where they congregate. However, just talking to millennials doesn't really accomplish the goal of making them reliable Republican voters. What does make them reliable Republican voters is bringing them into the fold by getting them engaged with the party apparatus, be it locally or nationally.

Millennials like to feel important and involved, which is exactly why we must treat them as more than just potential voters, donors, and volunteers. Each and every one of them should be considered a priceless commodity, which is why they must be treated as more than just a like or comment on a tweet or Facebook post. They seek validation.

In order to succeed digitally, Republicans must do more than just connect on social media. We must embrace big data and use it to determine how to craft messages, get out the vote, work to make campaigns more efficient and cost-effective, and bring new voters and supporters into the fold.

However, we cannot do this without following the examples of Obama's 2008 and 2012 presidential campaigns: Republicans must recruit top tech talent, which is primarily millennials, from Silicon Valley to revolutionize our digital operations. There exists a hurdle to this recruitment effort: the Republican Party is not a terribly enticing political party for millennials. Just like millennial voters in general, Silicon Valley tech talent will need to be won over and convinced to join the GOP because our ideas appeal to them. At present, Republican ideas are not terribly tempting or alluring, as they just don't sync up with the political views of millennials. This is partially due to the caricature of Republicans that has been created by Democrats and the media. It is also as a result of the GOP's failure to build an infrastructure to recruit this demographic. Were we to shift and adapt to Silicon Valley tech talent, we could attract this vital demographic. At the same time, Republicans can do so without sacrificing our conservative principles.

There is good news when it comes to Republicans building successfully on the Internet. The race for the 2016 Republican Presidential Nomination saw members of the Republican Party fracture and fight one another over Donald Trump's candidacy. By the time of the Nevada caucus in late February 2016, the hashtag #NeverTrump had emerged and was a way for conservatives that opposed Trump to organize across multiple digital platforms. They might have supported different conservative presidential candidates, but they all shared one common goal: derailing the campaign of Donald Trump. Soon, the website NeverTrump.com launched. The site served as an online petition for supporters to add their name to the list of Americans who opposed the candidacy of Donald Trump. In order to add one's name to that list, all a person had to do was to provide their name, email, and zip code. Thousands upon thousands did and, in the process, gave the site's organizer, the Never Trump PAC, their contact information. This contact information allowed the Never Trump PAC to organize the movement. It was not a party-wide movement (one could call it a micro movement), but large enough that it allowed Republican operatives to build their digital capabilities for the future.

Sure, the work and efforts of the anti-Trump forces were not on par with that of Barack Obama's presidential campaign of 2012 or even 2008, but it did provide the start of a foundation for conservatives across the United States. Further, Donald Trump's candidacy served as a potential gateway to groups that are typically dismissive of the GOP and its candidates. Republicans will need to use this resistance to Trump to demonstrate that the caricature of them is false.

Now, we must take the work of the Never Trump PAC and others, and use it to build the Republican Party for the fights and races it will encounter in the future.

Chapter 4
Charting a course

ONE OF MY MORE VIVID MEMORIES WITH MY DAD IS RIGHT AFTER I became politically active. We were driving to Costco for our regular father-and-son bulk-item-buying and for the free snacks available at the demo stations. We began talking about the education system in New York and teachers unions. As we got lost on our way to Costco, he began to tell me the story of a client he had represented who had a child with mental retardation and required a specialized private school in order to receive effective schooling. Under the law, because the public school system is not capable of providing these specialized services within their existing structure, the school system is legally required to pick up the tab of the private school. In this particular case, the child was potentially on the border of what was considered mentally handicapped. The school system opposed the parents' request that they pay for the specialized schooling; their claim was that the child was not mentally handicapped. This went where most things such as this end up: in court.

The court proceedings began and it came down to expert testimony. My dad decided to seek the opinion of the doctor who established the very criteria that New York City used to determine who is and who is not mentally handicapped. The doctor got on the stand and her own credentials were established with a series of questions. Next, she discussed how she had interviewed and tested the child and determined that the child was indeed a special-needs student. With that, the city's lawyer "turned pale" and the judge halted the proceedings to encourage the lawyer and my dad see if they could reach a quick settlement outside of the courtroom. It was clear to all that the city's opposition had just evaporated. The doctor's testimony had torpedoed the city's position.

This is where it got interesting. The city lawyer and my dad completed their conference outside the courtroom. They had quickly reached a settlement where New York City agreed to provide the funds needed for this child's private special-needs education. The two of them reentered the courtroom to find that the doctor—the expert witness—was still sitting on the witness stand. However, she was in tears and visibly distraught. What had happened during the five minutes that the lawyers were out of the room?

The doctor then told my dad the story of what had happened inside the courtroom once he left. A representative of the teachers union had stood up and walked to her. This teachers union official asked her why she was "betraying" her friends, the teachers. How could she do what she had just done?! Testifying in a way that supported this kid's case?! To them, it was an unthinkable betrayal. The union man then became more intense. "Don't you get it?! You're taking money out of our pockets!" He had tipped his and the teachers union's hand: the union wasn't looking out for this kid, or any other for that matter. What it cared about was how providing this child with the means to receive a proper education and care—means that were within the child's legal right—took money away from their local schools. The teachers union felt that the money was for them, not for the students. What a warped view to have of education funding.

The problems that are the root causes of the protests of Occupy Wall Street, Black Lives Matter, and the ones on college campuses are vast and took hold decades ago. Only now are the chickens coming home to roost. Republicans have the tools required to right these wrongs. Our policies can end the cycle of victimhood and spur education and innovation within inner cities. Unfortunately, there are a few impediments to achieving this. The surrender of urban areas by the party has hindered our ability to immediately get into the inner-city communities we want to help. However, the solution has been one that can be implemented without a Republican Party apparatus being in these areas right now. What we can't do without being directly in these neighborhoods and locales is take the credit for helping (some Democratic Party machine-elected stooge and opportunist will surely say they did it, when in reality they would fight the solution tooth and nail).

Returning to Joe Lhota, the 2013 New York City Republican mayoral candidate who became an advocate of inner-city minorities, we can see that there is a natural disconnect between Democrats and urban minorities on matters of education. Democrats repeatedly demonstrate that they are out of touch with the needs of students and their parents by kowtowing to the whims and desires of the teachers unions. These unions hold a tremendous amount of sway over Democrats and can literally pick up the phone and get their bought-and-paid-for elected officials to do their bidding. Teachers themselves are not the problem. Their unions are.

Lhota's decision to get involved in urban education issues, specifically access to charter schools (public schools that operate in a manner that allows innovation and accountability, while not being subject to the same limitations as other public schools) for minorities, was a smart one. As mentioned before, parents did a double take. A Republican supporting them?! Had hell just frozen over?! No, they found out that the people who Democrats portrayed as uncaring were surprisingly on their side. As march and rally participants repeatedly told reporters, they might not end up supporting Lhota in the general election, but they certainly would not vote for the Democratic alternative, Bill de Blasio, because he had a very close, public, and tight-knit relationship with the teachers union, the United Federation of Teachers. That's progress for the GOP.

Do charter schools increase opportunity and reduce inequality? Without a doubt, yes. Parents know this and are willing to do anything short of murder to ensure their child is granted admission and does not have to attend public school.

The National Charter School Study of 2013 published by the Center for Research on Education Outcomes found that charter schools overwhelmingly benefit minorities and the poor.[21] At the same time, study after study have clearly demonstrated that the poorest neighborhoods have the lowest-performing schools. This has been occurring for decades and it's no accident that Democrats—and by virtue, the teachers unions—have been in charge of these schools for decades.

Many academics have noted a correlation between the economic status of a neighborhood and the quality of education that that neighborhood receives—the poorer the neighborhood, the worse the quality of education.

Democrats often cite how education is the "silver bullet" when it comes to ending poverty. This is an absolutely true statement. The more educated a person is, the greater the number of work and life opportunities will be available to that person. The avenues of success are increased even further when the education that is provided and received is of the highest quality possible. Unfortunately, Democrats don't practice what they preach on education.

The Democratic Party and its office-holding members have their hearts in the right place on education, but when it comes time for Democrats to propose and implement an education policy that actually increases future opportunity, they don't. This is when they show that they are beholden to the teachers unions whose sole purpose of existence is to advocate for the ease and comfort of its membership: the teachers.

When these debates over education policy arise, the leaders of the teachers unions demand a seat at the table. In theory, the input of this union is good to have, as it brings the voice of teachers to the table. Teachers are uniquely able to provide detailed feedback on what has worked in the classroom and what has not. They can provide constructive feedback that would help schools thrive. However, when teachers union representatives join the education policy discussion, they advocate policies and procedures that only benefit the teachers they represent.

Propose longer school days that may increase a child's knowledge? The teachers unions will oppose it. Propose a system that requires teachers to have their job performance evaluated? The teachers unions will oppose it. Propose allowing parents to choose what schools their children can go to in order to provide the option of keeping kids out of failing schools? The teachers unions will oppose it. Propose providing merit-based pay to teachers? The teachers unions will oppose it. Propose eliminating teacher tenure so schools can replace badly performing teachers with better ones? The teachers unions will oppose it.

Any change or attempt at progress that is proposed will most likely meet stiff opposition from the teachers unions. Their leaders being given a seat at the table during important debates is akin to thinking a toddler is capable of negotiating a complex deal. The union leadership acts like a petulant child when it hears something they don't like. They pitch a fit, frantically wave their arms in the air, and rant about how unfairly they are being treated. Somehow, reforming the education system is dangerous to the teachers unions. To them, the status quo must be maintained at all costs, even if it means sacrificing the future potential of the very people they are truly meant to serve: their students.

It is clear that the pattern of behavior from the leadership of the teachers unions has disqualified them from being able to be legitimate and productive parts of the conversation on the future of education. Just because the union leadership is determined to stop the wheel of progress does not mean that we should jettison teachers from the conversation. Instead, Republicans should invite the actual teachers to do the talking. These teachers should not be union representatives, but high-quality educators that know the daily struggles of the education system. Sure, they can be members of the union, but they should come willing to put everything on the table. Doing so will demonstrate what Republicans have said all along: we respect teachers and believe they are vital components of education. Also, it sends a signal that we do not work with groups that are rigid and inflexible.

Now that the teachers are at the table, we will need to bring representatives of the parents, education experts, and lawmakers into the conversation, too. As these groups all get together, they should focus on the issues that matter.

Teacher tenure is the practice of granting permanent status to teachers who have worked for a minimum amount of time. Essentially, it makes them a protected class that cannot be removed from their position unless there is extraordinary cause. Even when this removal is warranted and completed, the built-in protections of teacher tenure make it so that it takes an incredibly long time to terminate the teacher's employment. In a perfect world, we would be able to eliminate teacher tenure in one broad stroke. However, reality makes this impossible.

Public support for teacher tenure is difficult to gauge. In 2005, Gallup found that half of Americans are not familiar with the practice. This was true of both Americans with children in grade school and Americans without. The more voters learn about it, the more they favor either extending the period required to earn tenure or even completely eliminating it. In 2015, a USC Dornsife/*Los Angeles Times* Poll found that over half of California residents believed that teacher tenure should be achieved after longer than the two years that were on the books. This same poll also found that Californians were in favor of giving schools greater ability to fire ineffective teachers. On top of that, they believe that teachers should not be protected by seniority, but by performance. This is evidence that Republicans and voters—in very blue California—have the same views on how teachers should be treated by schools. It is an opportunity for Republicans to make headway, especially in urban communities such as Los Angeles and San Francisco.

Dan Schnur, director of USC's Jesse M. Unruh Institute of Politics, said that the poll shows how voters

> . . . want to help teachers and support them . . . but they're also more than willing to take stronger steps to remove ineffective teachers from the classroom.[22]

In that same article, the *Los Angeles Times* detailed the polls results:

> In California, nearly half of voters surveyed in the USC Dornsife College of Letters, Arts and Sciences/*Los Angeles Times* poll favored a longer period to earn tenure than the two years granted under state law. Among those who favored some form of tenure, the largest group wanted teachers to earn it after seven to ten years. More than a third opposed any form of tenure.

Of course, the teachers unions responded to the USC Dornsife/*Los Angeles Times* Poll in a predictable manner. They attacked and tried to discredit the poll. Clearly, its results were a threat to them and the status quo that they seek to perpetuate.

In New York City, the teachers unions (in New York City's case, the United Federation of Teachers) have a major enemy: Success Academy Charter Schools. It boasts thirty-four schools across four of the five boroughs of New York City and serves eleven thousand students. Of these students, 76 percent are from low-income families and 93 percent are students of color. Their families can't afford to send them to a fancy private school, where some charge more than a year's salary in tuition. Success Academy Charter Schools does not charge parents a dime in tuition. This only enhances its appeal.

Do Success Academy Charter Schools perform similarly to New York City public schools? No. They vastly outperform New York City public schools and demonstrate their value. In fact, it wasn't only Success Academy Charter Schools that surpass New York's public schools, but most other charter schools do, too. These circumstances all contribute to the popularity of charter schools across New York.

One charter school network did not perform so well. It had opened in 2005, the year before Success Academy Charter Schools had come onto the scene. The UFT Charter School was created by then–United Federation of Teachers President Randi Weingarten (who later would go on to head the national teachers union, the American Federation of Teachers in 2008) who looked to counter arguments by Republicans and pro-charter school advocates that the teachers unions were detrimental to the education of children. From day one there were problems. The UFT Charter School exclusively used education policies that were championed by the teachers unions. As a result, the school and therefore the students struggled. Year after year the State of New York threatened to take away the UFT Charter School's accreditation, effectively shuttering it. Its performance among students was among the lowest of all charter schools in New York City for years. In February of 2015, it was quietly announced that the UFT Charter School would close its elementary and middle school at the end of the 2015 school year. Quietly, the UFT Charter School died a long-awaited death. By virtue of its total incompetence in management and oversight, the United Federation of Teachers successfully proved its critics right: teachers unions have no idea how to best educate the nation's children.

Let's return to the point made earlier about how the teachers unions should not be permitted a seat at the table. These union leaders are clearly not qualified to come in and be a part of the discussion about how to best educate American children. However, there are some qualified people who do deserve a seat at the table: the teachers themselves. Teachers unions have always said that they are the voice of the teachers, but teachers themselves are far more capable of providing valuable insight and analysis into the education system. Republican-elected officials should actively court and work with actual teachers and sideline their fat-cat union leaders. When you put the teachers, elected officials, parents, and education policy experts in a room to come up with a way to improve our education system, you will achieve some great results. Why? Because everyone is focused on what is best for the students, our children.

No child should ever be forced to attend a failing school. There are both good and bad schools in urban public education systems. Which one a student attends is often determined by where they live, and where they live is determined by the economic status of the parents. Democrats have taken the approach that instead of closing failing schools, they will seek to improve them. There is nothing wrong with wanting to improve a failing or subpar school, but this approach creates a problem: the students already in this failing school most likely won't receive the benefits of a quality education. As a result, they will ultimately be forced into a life of low-skilled careers and odd jobs. Yes, McDonald's and UPS need employees, but people should work for them because that is what they want to do, not because they were forced to attend a failing school that limited their life opportunities.

Republicans need to empower parents to make the choices regarding their children's education. They are the ones most-invested in the future of their kids, not some bureaucrat in the Department of Education who views each student as a statistic. We have long pushed for school choice, a policy that, among other things, gives parents vouchers to direct their child's share of their education tax dollars to a private school of their choice. However, that's a bit rigid and limits the choice of parents between public school and private school. It does not empower parents to access other educational tools that would benefit their children. This is where Education Savings Accounts (ESAs) come into play.

Education Savings Accounts are the new and improved school voucher. They empower parents to choose how their child's share of education spending is allocated. Parents can use the ESA to choose to continue to send their child to public school or enroll the child in private school, but where the real value of the Education Savings Account comes into play is with other educational options including tuition for private school, tutoring, services providing special education, homeschooling expenses, books, and many other services.

This raises an interesting option that should be pursued: online education. As a generation, millennials are more willing to conduct business via phone, teleconference, and email than prior generations.

Americans are not only using digital technologies to work from home or from their local Starbucks, but their doing so is openly accepted by both society and their employers. Why shouldn't education be the same way?

One barrier disadvantaged students face in education is access to the Internet. The *New York Times* pointed out in a February 2016 article that poorer families often view Internet access as a luxury expenditure that can rarely be afforded.[23] What little Internet access they have is often slow and cumbersome, which inhibits the child's ability to do work online. This creates a problem for the economically challenged student, as many schools are resorting to teaching using Internet resources. Increasing access to the Internet is paramount to ensuring a child has access to education and knowledge. It is also important because from millennials on down, younger Americans are incredibly connected to the Internet.

We must also remember that as generations change, so do the ways in which they choose to learn. As Northern Illinois University pointed out in its research paper on millennials and education, "Millennials: Our Newest Generation in Higher Education":

> Learning more closely resembles Nintendo than logic. Nintendo symbolizes a trial-and-error approach to solving problems; losing is the fastest way to mastering a game because losing represents learning.[24]

It is fair to say that this "Nintendo approach" to education that millennials have will be held by future generations as well. This method of thinking makes it imperative for us to gear our education policy and programs toward the very people it aims to serve. Of course, few to no millennials are still in grade and high school, but their children will be in the coming years. Their parents will raise them to use the same thought processes that they use. However, their version of this will be upgraded and enhanced through access to technologies that these children will grow up with (iPads, iPhones, etc.) and master before they get the ability to read (my nephews both knew how to use their parents' iPhones before they hit kindergarten). We will need to adapt our education system to be more trial-and-error facing.

Online education has suffered a few high-profile setbacks. In the past fifteen years, many online colleges have emerged and advertised how they will help Americans earn their degree at whatever pace they want. It sounded too good to be true and it was. Many of these online schools have been sued for fraud. In 2009, The University of Phoenix settled a class-action fraud lawsuit filed against them for $78.5 million.[25] It was alleged that the University of Phoenix had defrauded the United States Department of Education. This didn't help the reputation of online universities. Nor did Trump University, which, according to allegations in several well-publicized lawsuits, seemingly did not really have any educational value. However, some credible and accredited institutions, like George Washington University, have been forward thinking. They have offered master's degree programs that are entirely online.

What about if Republicans were to make it easier for accredited and reputable centers of education and universities to provide online education and distance learning? What if the GOP were to make it easier for students to take part in online education? We can. The Internal Revenue Service already offers education tax credits to Americans, so Republicans should move to provide tax credits for online education.

A major problem with education is how education standards are being set remotely from Washington, DC. This means that some faceless bureaucrat, who has no personal connection to the students or understanding of the daily circumstances they face, is making the decisions about what and how American children will learn. It has long been the position of the Republican Party that we should let parents and local educators set the educational agenda for our kids. They are the ones who are in touch with the needs and wants of our children. This is a path we should remain on as a party.

Schools, school districts, and education providers should be in the driver's seat when it comes to setting the agenda and standards that we teach to our children. This does not mean that each locale should be able to teach anything they like, such as revisionist history that denies evolution or some other lesson that is counter to fact. This means that the parameters for what to teach our kids are narrow enough to keep from teaching false or irrelevant lessons and wide enough to allow for freedom to tailor the curriculum to what works for each locale.

Providing educational opportunities to America's children will set them on the path to success. However, Democrats today have built a system that sets many urban residents on a path of failure. Republican educational alternatives, just a few of which are outlined above, can reverse and prevent this from happening. The evidence of the demand for real education opportunities is clearly demonstrated by the sheer demand among minorities in urban population centers.

Once these positive changes are put in place in order to serve and appeal to urban voters and millennials, the key is to ensure that they are able to move from high school to a college education. Unfortunately, a college education presents some problems for all Americans. These problems are not ones of educational quality (for the most part), but of affordability. We send our kids off and into college to prepare them for the world, but from the moment they arrive on campus for freshmen orientation, they are saddled with something they don't want: debt.

Chapter 5
I owe how much?!

WHAT REALLY FREAKS THE HELL OUT OF ANY GENERATION IS personal debt. Millennials graduate from college with an average of $31,000 in student debt. To put that in perspective, that's nearly two times the average American household credit card debt of $15,762.[26] Millennials are starting their adult lives in a state of indentured servitude to Sallie Mae, Chase, Bank of America, Wells Fargo, etc. Their starting salaries go toward paying down this crippling debt, when most millennials would rather it go to saving for a home, a fun vacation, or higher-quality beer.

The cost of living has also increased while American wages have remained stagnant. Daily costs have soared. Take, for example, the cost of a ride of a subway or bus in New York City. A one-way trip cost $2 in 2008. For a person to commute to work, it would cost at least $20 for a weekly commute and roughly $1,040 annually. At the start of 2016, the cost of a one-way trip on the New York City subway system was $2.75. That's $27.50 a week and $1,430 a year just to go to work. In eight short years, the cost of commuting to and from work has increased $390 a year, or 37.5 percent.

Have wages increased 37.5 percent? Nope. They have been relatively stagnant, which has made Americans angry and uneasy.

Americans have felt that there are more roadblocks to success and that America isn't what it used to be. President Obama and his surrogates repeatedly stress how great the economy is, but there is a real disconnect between the president and his people. The economy might be doing well overall, but it is not reflected in the daily lives of Americans. Who can blame their frustration?

Donald Trump entered the 2016 GOP presidential race on June 17, 2015, and quickly vaulted to the top of the polls through the sheer exploitation of the general unease that Republican voters felt. What his campaign did not offer were specific plans for solving the problems we face.

The Trump approach to fixing the economy? We're going to make some deals.

How? By making America great again.

His campaign lacked the reality and depth required of a serious candidate for president of the United States.

On the Democratic side of the 2016 presidential race, Senator Bernie Sanders of Vermont capitalized on this feeling and ran a populist campaign based on the redistribution of wealth and punishing the successful. It is counter to everything that the United States stands for. However, it does sound appealing to those receiving the short end of the stick when it comes to economic fairness. Sanders has told his supporters that the wealthy are to blame for their fiscal troubles and that he will be the one to punish them—a pretty radical platform. Yet, it is resonating with the voters because they feel left out. The American Dream feels more and more elusive. Previous generations could seize the day and become something. This generation . . . they are too busy living hand-to-mouth.

Bernie Sanders, everybody's crazy uncle, also played to the unease of Americans and worked to bring his outsider brand to the masses. Hitting on the central theme of income inequality, Sanders pushed his own brand of prescriptions on how to fix the United States.

He quickly became the candidate of the millennials and white urban voters in the Democratic Party. In the Iowa caucus, Sanders thoroughly trounced Hillary Clinton among millennials by a margin of 84 percent to 14 percent. The Sanders message clearly resonated among Democratic millennials and he won them over by a margin of 70 points in Iowa.

A more specific reason that Bernie Sanders scored big with millennials is that he directly addressed what, to them, was the elephant in the room: student debt. Again, an average of $31,000 in student debt is a large and daunting number that scares recent college graduates who will make just over $35,000 a year for their first post-college job. Sanders also went further and questioned student debt interest rates.

In February 2016, Bernie Sanders went even further and called for the student debt of a Columbia University graduate to be completely forgiven. At a rally in Manchester, New Hampshire, an audience member told Sanders that she faced a significant amount of student debt, some $200,000 worth. Sanders's response? Forgive the loans. That is perplexing. Using her own free will, the student chose to attend Columbia University and pay an average annual tuition of $49,138. In contrast, according to the College Board, the average annual rate of tuition of a public university $9,410, one-fifth of that of Columbia. The student had the right to choose the less expensive option of a public university (many of which provide high-quality education and valuable degrees), but chose to go with the option that was five times more expensive per year. It is clear that this student is a smart and intelligent woman. One can ascertain this fact just by seeing that she attended Columbia University. In making her decision to attend there, she must have been capable of calculating the cost. After all, she did get into Columbia. Student loan interest rates are not responsible for this woman's student debt. In fact, if you eliminated interest from student loans, it would not make the slightest bit of difference for this student. It's just window dressing and a

PR tactic to gain support, because nobody likes paying interest on any sort of loan.

The interest rates of student loans do not contribute to the high cost of college. It's well and good, but lowering them does not solve the problem of college affordability. The cost of tuition, textbooks, room and board, and other normal college expenditures would not be impacted one bit.

Another Democratic push is to make college tuition-free so that students wouldn't have to worry about leaving college with student debt. What an idea! If only reality didn't mean that these students who received the "free tuition" would actually have to pay for their college education in a less direct manner. In order to fulfill this Democratic Party initiative, taxes would have to be drastically increased on all taxpayers. When students would leave college, they would likely pay a higher tax rate than they do today and be just as economically crippled as they would be with $31,000 worth of student loans.

College is becoming increasingly unaffordable. So what can we do? There are a number of steps that Republicans can take to lower the cost of college. Significant reforms are desperately needed. The size and scope of the reforms required to lower the cost of college will scare many off. Naysayers will say that achieving results will be too difficult and daunting. Let's aim to prove them wrong.

One area not being discussed is the exorbitant salaries being paid to college coaches. Yes, it can be argued that it is the free market determining the value of these football and basketball coaches. Sure, Alabama's Nick Saban is a great football coach, but is he really worth $6,950,203 per year? At the same time, the average annual salary for a professor at the University of Alabama is $97,800. Clearly, professors should have been football coaches. By these numbers, it is a logical conclusion that coaches contribute to the affordability problem. College football and basketball are great and fun traditions. However, they are driving the cost of college up.

Another cause of increased college costs is the building of new college athletic facilities. The University of Oregon spent $68 million on a new athletic facility that was to be used exclusively by its football team. As far as academic facilities go, they are not being given the same level of attention that the football team is receiving. Oregon proposed a renovation to some facilities for students that would cost a total of $5 million. That is a far cry from the amount invested in the Oregon Ducks new football building. It is also important to not forget that many of these athletic facilities are being funded using taxpayer dollars. It is a costly investment in a facility that only a select few are allowed to use.

It is logical that we should seek to alter this disparity between academics and athletics. Few students are attending college to play sports, but all students are at college to learn. College students are essentially being forced to pay for a select minority to have the latest and greatest innovations for extracurricular athletic activities.

At the same time, this does not mean that all academic pursuits are valid or likely to provide intellectual nourishment to their students. Take University of Missouri communications professor Melissa Click who rose to notoriety during the protests in the fall of 2015. Her fifteen minutes of fame—or infamy rather—came when she told a student reporter he was not allowed to film her and other student protesters in a public space. When the reporter calmly informed her that he had the right to be there and to cover the story, Click called for other protesters to come over and remove the reporter with physical force. The entire incident was captured on film and went viral on social media.

In a twist of irony, a few days prior to Professor Click calling for the forcible ejection of the press, she had taken to Facebook and called for as many members of the media to come and cover the protests that were occurring on the campus of the University of Missouri. She cited how they were standing up to racism and that they needed to get the "incredible story" out to the press—a far cry from the press-barring person she was shown to be in the video.

So who exactly is Melissa Click and why is she important to the conversation about making college affordable? When Click's brush with infamy happened, many began to scrutinize what this communications professor actually teaches students. It was a bit weird that a communications professor, who would be presumed to know the First Amendment, would call for a reporter to be denied access to a story (by force no less). The more she was scrutinized, the more bizarre things came to light. Melissa Click taught classes on such vital topics as *Fifty Shades of Grey*, Lady Gaga, and the relationship between class and food in reality television.[27] For this work, she earned $57,798.26 a year. While it is nowhere near what college football coaches are making, this isn't the best use of resources by the University of Missouri.

Sure, some will argue that Melissa Click is just one professor teaching some courses on some rather irrelevant things. However, she is just one of many professors across the country that are paid to teach courses that have zero positive impact for somebody entering the American labor force. How many employers are looking to potentially hire someone to be able to thoroughly analyze the socioeconomic implications of *The Bachelor* on the middle class? The professors that teach these niche courses need to be paid but ultimately cause the higher cost of education that is passed onto all students.

What other less-than-necessary costs are being passed onto students? How about the University of North Florida that built a high-end lazy river for one of its dorms? Or the University of Texas, Austin, that has one dorm with actual maid service? These are but two of thousands of examples of crazy expenditures that public colleges are making. Each and every one of these amenities are luxuries financed by the taxpayer and/or the students of the university. They certainly aren't lowering tuition to pay for them. If these were private universities, it would be within their rights to build these facilities and pass the costs onto the students. Public universities have one duty: to provide the highest-quality education possible to their students. Their duty is not to give students the coolest pool, video game centers, or other extravagant recreational objects.

Personal debt is not the only debt that makes Americans uneasy. Government debt, now in excess of $19 trillion, is bad news for the United States. Who is going to be picking up the tab? Millennials. The president of the organization Generation Opportunity, Evan Feinberg, summed up the problem:

> Millennials were born free, but everywhere we're now in chains. The culprit is the skyrocketing national debt levels of the past decade, which have hurt young Americans and millennials more than anyone else. We're already facing enough personal debts as it is—and now we're being asked to pay for everyone else's.[28]

Wait a second, isn't the Republican Party the party of fiscal responsibility and restraint? Yes, it is. Then why did it allow the national debt to increase $4.899 trillion, a massive number, during the two terms that George W. Bush occupied the Oval Office?[29] Tough question to answer, especially given its complexity.

Let's refer back to Cincinnatus and the moral of that story. Power can be a corrupting influence that causes people to do things that are not in the national best interest. So in order to hold onto that power, lawmakers use the power of the purse to allocate funds to deliver for key interests and groups that are vital for reelection. There is nothing illegal about it, but it does contribute to excess spending of government funds.

President Bush allowed for spending to rise, but he also caused the increase in the deficit by creating an entirely new cabinet agency, the Department of Homeland Security, and launching two costly wars. All of these expenditures were necessary, but they were not exactly good for the fiscal health of the United States. Yet the spending of the Bush presidency is nothing compared to that of President Obama.

The national debt is expected to exceed $20 trillion by the time President Obama leaves office.[30] By the time he completes his second term, it will be almost double what it was when Obama first took office. In 2014, *Bloomberg* reported that the national debt per person in the United States was $58,604 (and that was when the national debt was just below $18 trillion). Lest we forget, that number has grown and is still growing. Even if every American were able to pay off the $58,604 related to each of them, further debt would be incurred due to the lack of spending cessation.

So now what are millennials supposed to think when they leave college with almost $90,000 in debt (student debt plus their share of the national debt)? It is a really depressing number to face when first entering the working world. This has primed millennials to be influenced by more fiscally responsible moves.

Democrats have always favored fixing problems by throwing good money after bad. Have a failing school? Increase its funding and that should fix the problem. It is not a responsible move to be made by any elected official. Republicans need to continue to highlight this as a practice that cannot be continued. However, this alone won't move the needle on the national debt. We will need to cut spending across the board, even to the military.

Republicans have long talked about what and how to do this. We've proposed balancing the federal budget so that the United States does not spend more than it takes in (which is the same practice as people perform in the average household). Chris Edwards, the director of tax policy at the CATO Institute, told the House Budget Committee that:

> Without major reforms, federal debt is expected to soar in coming years. CBO's "alternative scenario" shows that spending will grow from 20 percent today to 32 percent by 2040, while debt held by the public will grow from 74 percent to 170 percent.[31]

Republicans have long proposed major reforms, but the public support has not been there. Now, millennials present us with the opportunity to finally garner the public backing required to implement these needed reforms. Winning over their support, especially given how debt-conscious they are, would give congressional Republicans the leverage they require to push for real reform.

Leverage cannot be achieved without actively campaigning on the debt problems that plague the United States and its citizens. While Republicans have had a strong message on how to deal with the national debt, it clearly has not resonated with millennials and urban voters. Therefore, the GOP needs to refine the message.

One common part of the GOP's message on debt reform is the need to cut entitlements. This is not something that connects. Urban residents and millennials believe that entitlement programs are positive forces in the United States that exist to help the people. At the same time, millennials view entitlement programs, such as Social Security and Medicare, as having significant problems and not being effective in this day and age.

In 2014, entitlement programs were paid for with two-thirds of the federal budget.[32] By the end of 2021 entitlement programs will be paid for with 83 percent of the federal budget. This leaves 17 percent of the remaining federal budget to pay for everything else we need, including the military and other parts of our national defense. The percentage of the budget of entitlement programs won't stop increasing there. It is expected to grow and grow until it consumes 100 percent of the federal budget by 2033 (and it probably will keep growing).[33]

A 2011 study from the Pew Research Center about the 2012 election and the differing views of the generations, found nearly universal agreement among each generation when it came to the benefits of entitlements, but millennials did not feel that Social Security and Medicare were in good fiscal shape.

> When it comes to the two core entitlement programs serving seniors in America—Social Security and Medicare—there is broad consensus regarding their value to the nation as well as the precariousness of their finances.

> Nearly nine in ten Americans say each of these programs has been good for the country over the years, and this includes at least eight in ten across all generations young and old. Similarly, roughly three-quarters say these programs are in only fair or poor shape financially, and this view crosses generational lines as well.
>
> Where the generations differ is in their evaluations of the current effectiveness of these programs. Only members of the Silent Generation—the vast majority of whom receive Social Security and Medicare—say these programs do a good job of serving the people they cover. Majorities of millennials, generation Xers, and boomers say the programs do only a fair or poor job.[34]

Pew's study demonstrates that entitlement reform is needed, but there is no support for cutting funds to programs such as Medicare and Social Security. What is implied, however, is the desire to reform entitlements so that they are viable and accessible for future generations.

The Republican message needs to move forward to say that Medicare and Social Security are part of the foundations of American society. Talking about cuts only turns voters away. What should be talked about is improvement through reform. It is part of a pro-family and pro-individual agenda that the Republican Party stands for.

Chapter 6
You are entitled to nothing

THERE IS A HUGE AND LOOMING PROBLEM FOR MILLENNIALS: Social Security is not going to be around for them. In 2011, the nonpartisan Congressional Budget Office (CBO) warned that if we kept on the track that we are on now, Social Security will be completely drained by the year 2037. Yet, millennials are still forced to pay into the Social Security system and it makes them even more frustrated that it is in serious trouble. Medicare and Medicaid are also in peril. Every entitlement program faces major fiscal problems that threaten its existence for millennials. Reform is desperately needed and our elected leaders have not delivered much-needed fixes to major entitlement programs. In fact, they have chosen to ignore the problems and kick the can down the road.

First, Republicans must shed their fear of touching the so-called "third rail" of American politics and propose major reforms to the Social Security program. Raising the retirement age, which is anathema to the Democratic Party, is an essential part of this reform. Democrats repeatedly insist that raising the eligibility age for Social Security is some way in which the elderly are punished and forced to work longer.

In 1930, the average life expectancy of a man in the United States was fifty-eight years and for American women, it was sixty-two years. Those numbers have increased greatly. In 2014, American men had a life expectancy of 76.4 years and 81.2 for American women. As in life expectancy, the population of the United States has also increased since the 1930s. In 1935, 127.3 million people were in the United States. At the beginning of 2016, that number had nearly tripled with a population numbering 322.8 million people. That's a pretty big increase in the responsibility and strain on the Social Security system.

As the population of the United States and life expectancy of Americans grew, Social Security remained stagnant. It did not adapt to the situation that the country faced. At the time of Social Security's creation, most Americans were not expected to live to the age of eligibility to receive payments. From a financial standpoint, this was great for the federal government. As life expectancy grew, so did the cost of Social Security. The longer a person receiving Social Security lives, the more it costs the taxpayer. Today, life expectancy continues to increase while the requirements to receive Social Security remain unchanged.

It is no wonder that millennials look at their paystubs to see that 6.2 percent of their income was automatically deducted to pay for Social Security. The government frames it as an investment for the future, but it really is a way of sustaining a system that is on the brink. Millennials aren't stupid. They know that the chances of them seeing that money when they retire forty or more years later are slim to none. We see it as something way off in the distance that will have little to no impact on our retirement income.

Right now, Americans can begin collecting their Social Security benefits at the age of sixty-two. However, if they are willing to wait until age sixty-seven, their benefits will be increased by 6 percent. After this, the benefits increase 8 percent per year until age seventy.

A sensible and necessary reform would be to raise the Social Security eligibility age to seventy-two. This should be done for people who are under the age of fifty. If you are over fifty, then your retirement age should not change. Additionally, we must have the ability to revisit the policy in the future as the life expectancy of Americans goes up or down.

Raising the retirement age will meet resistance from Democrats. Why wouldn't they object? When Republicans talk about reforming Social Security, the Democrats hear some sort of alternate intent in their plans. When we say "raise the retirement age," Democrats hear "let's cut Social Security benefits" and/or "it's time to end entitlement programs." Raising the retirement age is not because we Republicans seek to cut benefits or end Social Security.

On the contrary, Republicans want to ensure that Social Security remains a viable and functioning part of the United States. Raising the age Americans need to be in order to receive Social Security benefits is not only fiscally responsible, it is essential.

There is another important way for Republicans to preserve and protect Social Security: means testing. Means testing is the system where Social Security benefits can be reduced for individuals with wealth who pay into the system, but clearly will not need to receive Social Security benefits. This is not taking away their benefits, but trimming them. It enables the Social Security Administration to save money and ensure that the neediest recipients will not have to worry about whether or not they will receive their benefits.

Democrats will scream bloody murder as Republicans attempt to move to implement Social Security means testing. If it were not so serious, it would be comical. Democratic candidates across the country are running for office on the platform of raising taxes on the wealthy, the very group of people who would see a reduction in Social Security benefits under means testing. Do they want to somehow tax all of their Social Security, too? They will have to recognize that this is a far more cost-effective way to pay for Social Security.

Medicare and Medicaid must also be reformed. Doing so would help to increase the health of Americans, as well as the overall quality of health care in the United States. Fixing and reforming these two health programs should come not from throwing more money to them, but by finding the problems that plague them and then mending them.

Take how Medicare and Medicaid have failed to embrace new technologies. As the economy has shifted to one of innovation and app-based services, the technology to receive health care via app has begun to take off. Gone are the days of having to call your doctor for help with noncritical medical issues. Telemedicine services that have health apps that enable you to receive medical care from your phone are a great innovation that positively impacts the health-care system.

Unfortunately, the federal government and the Center for Medicare and Medicaid Services (CMS) has thrown up a barrier to telemedicine services. Thirty-six percent of Americans are negatively impacted by this because they use Medicare and Medicaid. In New York State, 38 percent of its residents are hurt by CMS's antiquated policies. If you are one of these Americans and live in New York City, Boston, Chicago, Los Angeles, or another urban area, CMS only covers your medical care that involves you physically going to the doctor.

Why? Because government has been loath to embrace disruptive technologies such as telemedicine. In the view of CMS, you live close enough to many doctors, so telemedicine is a waste of government money and takes away patients from urban doctors. Nothing could be further from the truth. In fact, this just ends up making our health-care system less efficient and reduces the quality of care provided.

By examining the impact on New York City, we can see that it is important to change this outdated approach to telemedicine. Today, the average wait time to be seen in a New York City emergency room is over five hours. Once you are seen, you will face an average wait of a whopping twelve hours before you are discharged. Patients don't fare much better when it comes to seeing a primary care physician. They are subject to the mercy of the doctor's busy schedule and will not be able to get an appointment for at least a few days.

Telemedicine companies break down these impediments for you, the patient. You still receive the same high-quality care that you are looking for from a doctor and can get it 24/7.

A recent Kaiser Health study found that over a third of doctors no longer are accepting new Medicaid patients.[35] This, in turn, causes Medicaid users to resort to visiting the emergency room for minor ailments and injuries. The already astronomical wait time for all patients is further increased and hospital staff, doctors, and nurses are less able to provide personalized care to all patients.

In addition to the problems this backwards policy causes for doctors, nurses, and patients, it poses a massive fiscal problem for the taxpayer. The average cost of a visit to the emergency room in New York City is over $1,250. Yet only 4 percent of ER visits are for true critical care. The cost of using telemedicine for the same treatment is $50. This means that CMS is forcing New Yorkers and taxpayers to pay $1,200 more, a 2,400 percent markup, for care that can easily be handled by a telemedicine provider.

That's not fiscally responsible. That's taking a flamethrower to your tax dollars. Even the most ardent tax and spend liberals recoil at the wastefulness of this.

If CMS were to finally embrace new technology and cover telemedicine for urban Americans, the impact would be enormous and we would all be winners. This policy change would literally put no groups at a disadvantage.

First, patients would be able to have instant access to high-quality health care. Thirty-eight percent of New Yorkers and 36 percent of Americans would be able to immediately push a button on an app and be treated instantaneously. Gone is the need to go to the emergency room or primary care physician and taking time off from work or other events. You can be seen and treated in the time it takes to have a cup of coffee.

Next, emergency room wait times would be drastically reduced, as would the time it took to be released from the hospital. With fewer patients going to the ER to deal with minor ailments, the demand placed on the hospital is lessened.

This would also place less stress on doctors, nurses, and hospital staff by not having them rushing from patient to patient. With the increased time they can spend with each patient, they will be able to provide more personalized care, no matter what the ailment.

The benefits of telemedicine and health-care apps are clear. They increase accessibility to high-quality health care. They lower the cost of medical care. They relieve the stress placed on doctors, nurses, and other hospital staff. Most importantly, they reduce wait times at hospitals and doctors' offices. Who doesn't want this?

It's time for CMS to stop preventing Americans and urban residents from getting access to health care. It's time that doctors, nurses, and their staffs have less of a burden placed on them due to demand for treatment by patients. It's time we not overpay by $1,200 for medical care. It's time we cut the wait times in emergency rooms. Republicans should put pressure on CMS to open the door to telemedicine apps to 36 percent of the citizens of the United States whose Medicare and Medicaid plans do not cover it.

Medicare and Medicaid's reluctance to embrace new technologies is but one example of the overall problems they have when it comes to serving the public. In order to best serve Americans, we must push for the Center for Medicare and Medicaid Services to modernize and be able to allow for Americans to utilize new technologies in order to receive the lowest-cost but highest-quality care possible.

The millennial generation is one of independent self-starters. This generation is increasingly turning toward creating their own opportunities and businesses that enable them to pursue their passions. The idea of work being a source of misery has pushed them to pursue leisure through work they enjoy. This is setting the situation where millennials are buying their own health insurance plans instead of receiving them from employers under their employee group plans. Now, this creates a problem down the line. In fact, this future problem is a current problem for Americans turning sixty-five. If you turn sixty-five and do not receive your health insurance from your employer's group plan, you are required to enroll in Medicare Part A (free of charge) and can also pay a small premium to enroll in Medicare Part B.

Each and every time a Medicare recipient visits the doctor, Medicare will cover this medical appointment and the costs of subsequent treatment related to the ailment. Medical costs are through the roof already, so whatever money the Medicare recipient is paying for the Part B plan is about as impactful as using a squirt gun to put out a house fire. Without question, the government is saying that people sixty-five and older must be forced into a system that costs taxpayers more because there are no alternative options.

Doctors in New York City are loath to take Medicare. They despise how it reimburses for the treatment and care that they provide their patients. So it is not entirely shocking to learn that many people that are sixty-five and up wish that they had the option to pay for private health insurance out of their own pocket. Democrats are denying them that choice.

This must be changed. Republicans must act to empower Americans across the country to be able to make the choice to buy private health insurance when they reach the age of sixty-five. The denial of their right to choose how their own health care is provided is stunning. Democrats have been more than happy to let this policy be the status quo. In this case, they are against allowing American citizens the ability to make their own decisions about their own health care. Ironically, Democrats often call Republicans "the anti-choice party."

If older Americans want to enroll in Medicare as their primary means of health insurance, that is their right and privilege. They are more than welcome to do this. However, Americans who want to enroll in Medicare should do so because they believe it is better for them and their own medical needs to choose Medicare over private insurance.

The cost savings of this simple change would be enormous and could be another way in which we can cut our out-of-control spending. This would extend the life span of these programs and make them more than a foreign concept in the eyes of millennials.

Entitlements are not programs that Americans of any stripe want to eliminate. They are vital institutions that are part of the fabric of America. They will need to be reformed in order to be effective and survive.

Chapter 7
Focus on the family

WHAT IF THE GOP DID SOMETHING COMPLETELY UNORTHODOX and unexpected? What if they went out and tried to engage millennials in a manner that challenged Democrats on their own turf and used their own issues? Imagine how utterly perplexed liberals would be if conservatives worked to beat them on the matters that they champion. Further, imagine their reaction if we sought to use conservative values as our reason to do so. Their heads would explode.

Unlike prior generations, millennials seek a work-life balance and don't see any reason to work longer than a forty-hour work-week, especially when they are not compensated for extra hours in jobs that pay an annual salary. They further believe that the policy of paid family leave is a valuable commodity that helps to provide a more flexible and better work/life balance. Paid parental leave provides paid time off from work in order to care for a child.

Businesses are being told to adapt for the modern millennial workforce. These suggestions are coming not just from left-leaning groups, but also major corporations. Ernst & Young advised businesses to provide paid family leave to their employees, as a survey they conducted found that 86 percent of millennials are less likely to leave their job if paid family leave is offered.

If you are a business that has millennial employees, but don't offer paid family leave, then you have a big issue. With each and every millennial employee, there is a nearly 90 percent chance that they are looking to leave and move on. As their eyes scan job postings online at work, their productivity will suffer. When their productivity suffers, your company or organization's bottom line will suffer. The simple lesson for employers is that employees need incentive and motivation to be invested in the place they work. Paid family leave is one way to increase employee morale and satisfaction.

Most employers currently offer short-term unpaid family leave. It is neither sufficient nor economically viable for this policy to continue. In essence, it penalizes employees for having children and is far from pro-family. Is that something really worthy of us continuing?

Now comes the part where Republicans can co-opt the issue of paid family leave into party growth. Doing so would not betray our conservative values, but only enhance them. The family is integral to the fabric of America and its values. We want to provide strong and positive environments for our children to grow up in, not to mention to have the flexibility for their parents to be a part of their lives at birth or any point that they become sick.

At the same time, there will be natural resistance to the idea within the conservative ranks, as it can be seen as another way in which the government is inserting itself into the daily operations of a private business. Yet, conservatives helped pass the Family and Medical Leave Act, which President Clinton signed into law in 1993. The law ensured that workers could receive up to twelve weeks of unpaid leave.

Sure, many will have the knee-jerk reaction that this is a federal mandate. On the surface, it certainly appears to be counter to conservative values of small government, but what do we get if we fight for it?

First, millennials and urban voters will see this move as a surprise. Time and time again they've been told by the left and the media that we Republicans are anti-worker and pro-big business. Republicans oppose raising the minimum wage to $15 an hour, so why wouldn't they logically oppose paid family leave?

The Manhattan Institute's Kay Hymowitz noted that the Family and Medical Leave Act made exceptions for businesses:

> It didn't include companies with fewer than fifty on the payroll, and it only applied to workers who have been at the same firm for a year. It was also unpaid, meaning there were no direct costs to businesses and no new taxes.[36]

If Republicans can help a Democratic president pass the Family and Medical Leave Act with exceptions that protect businesses, then there is zero reason that we should not do so when it comes to paid family leave.

Remember, millennials are the largest part of the labor force in the United States and this is an issue that they deeply care about.

There is a side benefit to supporting paid family leave. Seventy-one percent of mothers are in the labor force, so allowing them the opportunity to take care of a child, when needed, will be quite welcome. This takes another talking point away from Democrats. They can't argue that Republicans have a "war on women" if the Republicans are actively promoting a pro-woman agenda.

Further, we can expand paid family leave's definition to include the ability for men to take paternity leave and workers to take leave in order to provide care to any family member, whether it is a child or parent, when they are ill. This expands the policy to any worker (and doesn't provide fewer benefits for people who decide not to have children). It's a compassionate and moral position to take—not to mention politically smart.

There is no doubt that supporting paid family leave would be a gamble. Democrats would try to celebrate this and claim the moral high ground. If they did that, it does not mean that they are correct. At the same time, small government Republicans would be somewhat troubled by what they saw as an expansion in government reach, but this "expansion" is nothing that Republicans should be concerned about, as paid family leave does not mean government overreach.

In order to avoid the charge of government getting too large with the issue of paid family leave, protections must be built into the law that allow certain businesses, essentially small businesses, to be exempt from the law.

Would it be fair to the company of ten people? If one of these ten workers were to take time off to have a child or care for a sick relative, the business would be responsible for paying the worker during his or her leave. At the same time, it would be hard on the other nine employees to absorb the duties of their coworker, so their employer would have to hire a temporary replacement. The replacement would cost this company more without offering more of a product to offer its customers. This very situation is why exemptions and protections must be built into paid family leave.

At the same time, businesses can be encouraged to offer paid family leave amenities, such as employers offering to set aside a program where employees contribute to an insurance plan via paycheck deduction. This insurance plan would be provided by a private insurance company and cover situations where paid family leave would be necessary. The insurance policies could offer varying degrees of coverage, so that people who take time off to care for a relative would be eligible to receive some form of compensation from the insurance company when they make use of paid family leave.

There are other areas in which we can promote the family, as well as single people. The Earned Income Tax Credit and Child Tax Credit both are ideas that offer economic empowerment. The problem is that their own complexities have made them difficult to effectively market and package to the public. The Earned Income

Tax Credit is a tax credit that not only gives low-to moderate-income Americans a tax cut, in some circumstances it even gives them a refund.

One issue is not really being discussed by either party, despite its importance and impact on Americans throughout the country. The system that provides care for older Americans is in shambles. Forget the problems with Social Security, Medicare, and Medicaid; the actual care for older Americans needs fixing.

The oldest Americans require care as they reach the end of their lives. Assistance varying from part-time to full-time is most likely necessary for most senior citizens. It could be something as simple as having somebody check in on them every now and then or be as complex as full-time care, as they might not be able to function on their own. The cost of this is a financial drain and burden on not only the person being cared for, but their families who help them out. The wealthiest Americans have the financial wherewithal to afford to send their grandparents or other older relations to nursing homes, live-in care facilities, or to provide them with some other form of care. The middle class has the ability to plan ahead (provided they have the foresight to do so) and figure out a way to establish a trust so that assets bypass probate court. Another advance planning option for the middle class is to develop an estate plan with an attorney so that assets, not costs of care, can be passed on to the next generation.

A report released in 2015 by Genworth Financial found that the median annual cost of a single private room in a nursing home in the United States is now $91,250. The cost of just one year in an assisted-living facility is not as severe as a nursing home, but still a daunting $43,200. How many Americans can afford this? Few have the financial resources to be able to provide for the adequate care needed for older or ill relatives.[37] So what are Americans to do when their parents or grandparents need care?

An increasingly common scenario is now happening across the country. Americans, particularly women, opting to avoid incurring the mammoth costs of assisted-living facilities and nursing homes, instead are becoming the care providers themselves. They either leave their jobs or take on positions that are offer fewer hours and therefore less pay. People who do this are not compensated for the care they provide. Forty-four million people care for the elderly in some function in the United States and do so in an unpaid capacity.[38] The AARP estimates that the United States economy loses $33 billion annually due to people removing themselves from the workforce to care for the elderly.

The MetLife Study of Caregiving Costs to Working Caregivers made some astounding and alarming findings:

- The total estimated aggregate lost wages, pension, and Social Security benefits of these caregivers of parents is nearly $3 trillion.
- For women, the total individual amount of lost wages due to leaving the labor force early and/or reduced hours of work because of caregiving responsibilities equals $142,693. The estimated impact of caregiving on lost Social Security benefits is $131,351. A very conservative estimated impact on pensions is approximately $50,000. Thus, in total, the cost impact of caregiving on the individual female caregiver in terms of lost wages and Social Security benefits equals $324,044.
- For men, the total individual amount of lost wages due to leaving the labor force early and/or reduced hours of work because of caregiving responsibilities equals $89,107. The estimated impact of caregiving on lost Social Security benefits is $144,609. Adding in a conservative estimate of the impact on pensions at $50,000, the total impact equals $283,716 for men, or $303,880 for the average male or female caregiver 50+ who cares for a parent.[39]

This study clearly highlights some of the many problems confronting Americans when it comes to caring for elderly relatives. Men and women across the country are sacrificing their own financial security and futures in order to care for their parents and grandparents. What happens to them when they try to reenter the workforce? It's already difficult enough in this country to get a good job when you are in your late forties on. There is also the issue of how many women take jobs where they have diminished salaries, roles, and time requirements in order to receive the flexibility required to care for their parents or grandparents. Certainly, a case could be made that this negatively impacts pay equity.

With baby boomers entering the age of retirement, the number of elderly Americans requiring some sort of care is expected to increase drastically. By 2030, the United States will need between 5.7 million and 6.6 million caregivers in order to take care of the expanding population of elderly Americans. It is expected that many of these caregivers will be relatives that remove themselves from the workforce in order to provide care. It's a recipe for economic disaster, as fewer Americans will be helping the economy to grow.

So how do we stop this? Why not combine this and the paid family leave insurance program solution? The insurance companies providing these policies could establish plans that will also cover the costs of caring for an elderly relative. This would allow for Americans to have legitimate and viable options for elder care. They could use this insurance to provide their parent or dependent with a paid and professional caregiver, an assisted-living facility, or even a nursing home. At the same time, this enables them to not only stay at their jobs, but to continue to climb the career ladder and avoid taking excess time away from the workforce and becoming essentially unemployable. Implementing this would have a significant positive economic impact on the United States.

Chapter 8
Netflix and chill?

THERE IS NO MORE IMPORTANT THING TO A MILLENNIAL THAN access to information from a digital platform. It is the vital link that we have to the world. If we millennials can't check our email, tweets, Facebook posts, and watch Netflix as desired, then we are not happy. Hell, the public service announcements about not texting while driving or crossing the street were practically designed for millennials. This isn't said to belittle or mock us; it is simply a fact. We really love being connected all the time and want that Internet connection to be lightning fast.

All Americans know and dread the "pinwheel of purgatory." This is when the television show or movie we are trying to stream is unable to play because it is buffering due to slow Internet speeds. It is one of the most aggravating first-world problems around. So when Internet providers wanted to charge their customers and other companies for the right to *not* have the speed at which videos are slowed or "throttled" down, consumers were justifiably upset. This wouldn't have just impacted streaming video, but would have slowed down online Call of Duty games and made many websites so slow to load that older millennials would think that they were back to using a dial-up modem.

Nothing could unite the millennial factions of the right and left like the issue of somebody holding their Internet access hostage in exchange for money. Republicans, who the left has long accused of being tools of corporations and "big business," showed themselves to be anything but, fighting efforts that would allow Internet providers to throttle down the Internet. Millennials in particular chafed at the idea that a company would be so greedy that it would charge users to access certain material at a speed greater than a snail's pace.

For several years, communications corporations pushed the idea that the Federal Communications Commission (FCC) had no authority to regulate the service that they provide, as they were not providing an "information service." The FCC pushed a controversial proposal that would allow broadband providers to create an "Internet fast lane" that would enable select Internet traffic to pass through this lane at a faster rate than regular Internet access.[40] This so-called "fast lane" would open the door to corporations to charge consumers for viewing content that the corporation chooses. Such content could be a rival's website or information that does not reflect positively on them. There is also the possibility that a broadband or telecommunications company would use such power in an irresponsible and punitive manner.

Imagine that telecom company Verizon feels that some of the media coverage they have received from reporters at the *Wall Street Journal* has been biased against them. In order to get payback and to send a message to other media outlets that are thinking about publishing less than flattering reports on them, Verizon just needs to designate the *Wall Street Journal* as being part of this "fast lane" that they are charging consumers extra to access, resulting in lower readership and subscription revenue. It is a rather scary power for a company to hold. It is our responsibility as Republicans and as Americans to protect consumers from this abuse of power.

Why should Republicans get into a fight over what essentially makes them seem pro-regulation, supporting the heavy hand of government? Because this is not really a fight over regulation or government having its fingers in the operations of a company. What this really comes down to is equality. Americans should be able to have equal access to the Internet and the sites they visit. Broadband and telecommunication companies should not have the right to discriminate against an audience based upon their preference of where they visit on the web or what apps they choose to use. It also would enable broadband companies to effectively violate free speech.

Republicans must work to protect the consumer from unequal treatment when it comes to the Internet. In 2015, the Federal Communications Commission adopted Net Neutrality by a three to two vote that was cast along party lines with Democrats in the majority.[41] The two Republican appointees to the FCC got their decision wrong. While the decision by the Federal Communications Commission was largely celebrated, as it deserves to be, some language in the rules now opens the door for free speech to be stymied through censorship and government regulation.

The issue of online censorship is fast becoming a hot and pressing topic. First, it was the kids who protested at their colleges in 2015. They pushed for "safe spaces" where they could be free from what they deemed to be hurtful speech. Now, online communities are cracking down on speech that some see as offensive. There are two famous examples of this.

The first involved Instagram, the photo-sharing app that was acquired by Facebook. Many women found their posts were being taken down because they happened to show their nipple in a picture. They found this to be a double standard, as men could post shirtless pictures that showed their nipples and face zero repercussions. Soon, millennial women started the hashtag freethenipple that sought to raise awareness of this problem. Women in New York City are allowed to walk down the street topless, so why shouldn't they be allowed to do the same on Instagram?

There are more and more instances of censorship and potential censorship of the Internet and the digital platforms where we coexist.

For the second example, Protect Internet Freedom, a group dedicated to the defense of a free and open Internet noted that:

> Recently, Google, Twitter, and other corporate tech giants that strongly favored the FCC assuming the role of government "referee" to ostensibly protect a "free and open Internet," are partnering with the German government to delete comments within twenty-four hours that the government deems cross the line. Under the agreement, even speech that is simply considered "insulting" to the government censors will be taken down.[42]

Now, in the age of college students protesting the slightest thing that they feel is offensive, Twitter and other companies are establishing systems that hinder free speech. In February 2016, Twitter announced the creation of Twitter Trust & Safety Council, what effectively was a form of censorship.[43] This council was to be composed of outside groups that were experts in their particular fields. They were being given the power to play umpire when it comes to each and every tweet. If a tweet were deemed to be offensive or even had the potential to hurt a person's feelings, then the Twitter Trust & Safety Council could act to save the day or something.

Remember, Twitter announced this only a few months after college campuses erupted in protests over perceived slights or "microagressions" that saw students thinking the use of the terms "freshman" and "sophomore" were somehow offensive. The speech they are targeting is not speech that should actually be reviewed and dealt with like actual threats. If somebody threatens to harm, rape, or kill another or themselves, of course Twitter and its users should immediately act and report that to the authorities. The same applies if a person appears to be contemplating self-harm. This is the extent of which there should be banned speech.

What happens if somebody tweets about the New York Yankees? A simple and inoffensive tweet of "I can't believe the Yanks lost to the Indians last night. Damn," has at least two things that some might feel are microaggressions. First, referring to the Yanks as Yanks could very well be reported for being insulting to the heritage of Southerners who had relatives that fought for the Confederacy in the Civil War. Then, referring to the baseball team from Cleveland, the Indians, is going to upset people with Native American ancestry and people from India. So offensive is this tweet that it surely will send hundreds of thousands of people into therapy in order to recover from the mental trauma of its insensitivity.

This is but only the tip of the iceberg. In 2016, Twitter enabled its millions of users to report tweets and content that most likely do not meet the criteria of offensive remarks. Twitter users were permitted to report speech as offensive because it is in "disagreement with my opinion" and little more.[44]

Censorship is a dangerous tool, especially online. It goes against every single thing that the Internet stands for. The Internet is for the free exchange of ideas and knowledge (and yes, it's also for the dissemination of cats that look pissed off). Restricting speech on digital platforms and the Internet is the wrong way to go about protecting yourself from material that a person deems objectionable. Users should know that there are many alternatives to the Twitter Trust & Safety Council. They include:

- Simply not being a part of Twitter.
- Not following potentially offensive accounts.
- Growing the hell up.

It is a safe bet that other digital platforms will follow Twitter's lead and begin trying to provide "virtual safe spaces" for people.

Facebook, Instagram, Snapchat, and many more could wind up losing what made them popular: free speech.

But wait . . . Twitter is a private corporation, so it is not a conservative approach to interfere with the internal operations and policies of a private business. If anything, doing so sounds like a liberal Democrat's standard platform of micromanagement and control. The charge is exactly right. The example of Twitter and its extreme censorship of its own users is one that needs to be considered in the light of Twitter and its relationship with the government.

Under Net Neutrality, the federal government was able to gain the ability to restrict and censor speech on the Internet. As a result, an unelected government official or bureaucrat can unilaterally tell a private Internet corporation to remove content from its site and/or platform. This can be done without going through any judicial review or formal process. Essentially, the government now can violate a person's First Amendment rights and force a company to be an accomplice to this constitutional violation. Why? Because Net Neutrality was anything but.

Where do Republicans need to stand on matters of the Internet and digital platforms? Simply, we need to stand on the side of protecting its openness and lack of heavy-handed intervention. Millennials overwhelmingly believe that the Internet should be left alone and allowed to be completely open and free. Evan Feinberg wrote in *Roll Call* in September 2014:

> Millennials who have witnessed the transformative power of a free Internet find it unfathomable that bureaucrats would consider breaking it. Internet freedom has driven progress in nearly every sector of our economy, immeasurably improving the lives of every American citizen.[45]

The quickest way to alienate millennials is to restrict Internet freedom. Companies and people own particular websites and digital platforms, but nobody owns the right to visit or censor them.

Ensuring that this remains the case is imperative to keep the millennial vote. Look at how people mobilized after comedian John Oliver highlighted Net Neutrality on his show, *Last Week Tonight with John Oliver*. Over forty-five thousand Americans left comments on the FCC's website (never mind the part he highlighted is actually an issue for the FTC because it involves commerce and trade, not communication) when Oliver asked them to in his short segment that aired at 11:00 p.m. on a pay cable channel on a Sunday night. It is fair to assume that few baby boomers were watching at this time. So strong was the response of Oliver's audience that they literally crashed the FCC's website (also showing that the FCC needs to modernize its site).[46] Heaven help the government agency or lawmaker who really pisses off people when more people are tuned in.

Pushing for a free and open Internet falls exactly within the ideals and values of the Republican Party. Additionally, it is in keeping with the views of older millennials and urban voters who champion the freedom of speech. Many Americans say they believe in free speech and that it makes up their core principles. That is something many say when they cite these fundamentals in situations when it is convenient. Principles and beliefs are only those when we stand by them when it is inconvenient. So fighting for free speech on the Internet is vital, even if the very speech were something that we could find objectionable.

The ultimate example of this is the 1989 Supreme Court case *Texas v. Johnson, 491 US 397* that affirmed by a vote of five to four that burning the American flag was a form of protected speech.[47] Who voted in the majority? The late Justice Antonin Scalia, the conservative firebrand of the Supreme Court. Not one of the justices who heard that case liked the idea of burning an American flag, the symbol of our great nation. Yet, the Supreme Court ruled that despite it being offensive, it was a form of speech and thus protected under the Constitution. Writing for the majority, Justice William J. Brennan stated:

> If there is a bedrock principle underlying the First Amendment, it is that the government may not prohibit the expression of an idea simply because society finds the idea itself offensive or disagreeable.

Republicans must view this decision as the gold standard of free speech, especially when it comes to the Internet. We must apply this decision not only to government, but private businesses, such as digital platforms, that promote the sharing of knowledge, expression, and ideas. It is imperative that we allow the Internet to grow and thrive, while ensuring that it is free from corporate or governmental interference. Such interference could come in the form of limitations of speech or in limitations of actual access to the content one wishes to access online. This also can cause a significant roadblock to innovation and economic progress. Millennials are using the Internet to create companies and products that "disrupt" traditional markets. With interference, this would be made even more difficult and stifle opportunity.

The Internet and the rise of smartphones have given rise to today's on-demand economy. Technology companies that provide services to consumers, such as Uber, have spurred innovation, created jobs, and disrupted industries for the better. Overall, they have had a positive impact on the places and people that they serve, which has earned them the loyalty and business of customers. It is a solid example of the free market working properly. However, there are some forces that would prefer that these companies not be successful.

In 2015, New York City was quickly becoming the biggest market in the world for the car service, Uber. Its unique and enticing draw that set it apart from other car services is that it is entirely managed via their app. In this app, the rider pushes a button, a car picks them up within minutes, takes them to their destination, and then charges the credit card that they have on file. It's fast, efficient, and simple, which is exactly what consumers want. New Yorkers loved it, but a small minority of them did not and set out to stop Uber's growth.

The yellow taxi is synonymous with New York City. It is a staple and constant presence on the streets of the city. So Uber's meteoric rise to popularity and mainstream use came at the expense of the old yellow taxi industry. The owners of the valuable taxi medallions realized the threat and began to call politicians to ask for "protection." This desired "protection" did not come out of some noble desire to save an industry that was essentially evolving for the better because of Uber. What it came from was a desire to not lose money at the hands of a competitor. Taxi medallion owners were calling the Democratic politicians, the majority of whom they had donated copious amounts of money to, and asking them to preserve their monopoly on the taxi industry.

New York City's Democrats sprang into action to do the bidding of their donors, the taxi medallion owners. Mayor Bill de Blasio soon began pushing a proposal that would cap the growth of Uber by restricting the number of cars and drivers it could have in its fleet. De Blasio and progressive members of the New York City Council set out to do this under the smoke screen of helping to prevent congestion on New York City's streets. Of course, there was no evidence that Uber caused increased traffic in the city, but de Blasio and Democrats pressed on regardless.

Then New Yorkers began their revolt. Sixty-five percent of New Yorkers said that they believed Mayor de Blasio's push to limit Uber was because he was acting in the interests of his donors and not the city that he was elected to govern.[48] New York City residents of all backgrounds began to speak up and voice their opposition to de Blasio's desire to cap Uber's growth. The prominent local news anchor, Errol Louis, penned an editorial in the *New York Daily News* which highlighted how Uber was a positive solution to a long-standing problem that many African American New Yorkers faced: discrimination at the hands of cab drivers.

> Yellow taxis ignore the boroughs where the vast majority of city residents live, and regularly violate the law by simply refusing to take passengers to the Bronx, Queens, Brooklyn and Staten Island. For my family, Uber is a godsend.[49]

Louis, who is African American, used this editorial to describe how African Americans were being treated equally by Uber and its drivers. They no longer had to worry about yellow cab drivers refusing them service, as they no longer needed to use yellow cabs. Uber and other car service apps were the solution.

Uber did not take de Blasio's threat to their business lying down. They launched a major public relations campaign and spent millions of dollars to keep de Blasio from running them out of town. The future of their company was at stake—if they were forced out of the New York City market, it would be a fatal blow to their company. They launched a series of ads, both on television and on digital platforms, that emphasized Uber's positive impact on its customers, particularly for those of color. No company had gone to war with a city like Uber had with New York.

Soon de Blasio's approval rating dipped as the Uber fight took its toll. De Blasio and Uber announced a "compromise" where the city agreed to study whether or not Uber impacted New York City traffic. Spoiler alert: that report was released in January 2016 and found that Uber had no impact on traffic in New York City.[50] De Blasio retreated and abandoned the fight.

Uber is just one company that is innovating and disrupting traditional industries. Many more companies across the country are changing the way in which their respective sectors work. Of course, they too are meeting opposition from the traditional companies that they are challenging. They are like Uber in that they are making their own trades better and more consumer friendly. They are not like Uber in that they cannot afford to spend millions of dollars to protect themselves from Democrats who want to stop their growth and protect their donors.

Again, government interference, be it at the hands of a bumbling mayor or a bloated and ineffective government agency, stifles growth. Thankfully, government has the ability to do some good by both backing off and creating the conditions required for a positive growth environment for its citizens.

As discussed earlier, education is the silver bullet to ending inequality and providing opportunity for all. However, many lower-income families face the barrier of a lack of access to low-cost broadband Internet. This hinders the educational opportunities and learning ability of students that have to overcome hurdles in order to get high-speed access to the web.

The Pew Research Center found in its December 2015 report, Home Broadband 2015, that Americans understand the benefits of high-speed broadband access, but also are cognizant of the fiscal constraints which it can place on a home.

- Roughly two-thirds (69 percent) of Americans indicate that not having a home high-speed Internet connection would be a major disadvantage to finding a job, getting health information, or accessing other key information—up from 56 percent who said this in 2010.
- Among non-broadband adopters, 33 percent cite the monthly cost of service as the main reason they lack broadband at home, with an additional 10 percent citing the cost of a computer as their main reason for not having broadband service.[51]

It is clear that we must ensure that high-speed broadband Internet access is more accessible and affordable for all Americans. Doing so is only a net positive for the United States and its citizens. So how do we make this a reality?

Many Democrats have pushed for American cities to build and implement free Wi-Fi hot spots so that city residents can have access to the Internet outside of their homes. In New York City, pay phones on the street are being converted into free Wi-Fi hot spots.[52]

Hillary Clinton proposed giving all Americans access to high-speed broadband by 2020. These are both good ideas in theory. However, they each have drawbacks that make them unworkable. In the case of New York City, making Wi-Fi free is not something that we should support. Like Bernie Sanders saying that he wants to make college tuition and debt free, this has hidden costs that will be passed onto the taxpayer. These free Wi-Fi hot spots for the public will be paid for by tax dollars (in addition to the corporate sponsors and advertising) and take away from other programs. Hillary Clinton's plan would cost the United States $275 billion, a sum that we can ill-afford.[53] There should be a more viable alternative that Republicans should champion.

The question of how to address providing high-speed Internet access to urban residents, while avoiding putting the taxpayer on the hook for the bill, is a difficult one. Many believe that there are two options to providing low-cost broadband access to urban residents. One choice is for the government to be the provider and manager/overseer. This approach bloats the responsible government's budget while requiring that they add staff to oversee and maintain the system. It should come as no surprise that governments are not the best at maintaining complex Internet services . . . or even websites.[54]

The other option is to have the government outsource all aspects of installation and maintenance to a private corporation. That corporation would install the broadband system and Wi-Fi hot spots, allow city leaders to take credit for it, then have the rights to oversee the network, which includes setting prices. This generally results in the company that administers the broadband system setting prices for access and ultimately charging consumers a rate that does not make these services more affordable. This can be a downside to the free market.

Yet, there is a third way to accomplish this. One that does not cause taxpayers to be on the hook for an astronomical sum of money, does not increase the size of government, and does not make the service(s) unaffordable to the consumer. It is the path that Republicans should take to ensure that we can thread that needle to avoid negative consequences. This is where the GOP should encourage companies such as Google (which already is investing in building a massive broadband network called Google Fiber) to provide broadband access to low-income and urban Americans. The encouragement should come from tax cuts that provide incentives to Internet providers to install broadband networks in low-income neighborhoods and public housing. Google has already partnered with the Department of Housing and Urban Development to do this in every public housing project across the United States.[55] Whether or not this federal effort will be successful is anybody's guess, but urban Republicans can push initiatives at the local level to help meet this goal.

Ensuring that Americans have access to low-cost high-speed broadband is a way for Americans to have increased opportunities and ability to pull themselves up by their bootstraps. Armed with the information found online, the possibilities for advancement are endless. With the information that one can procure online, millennials can find the latest news on Buzzfeed, reviews of the new bar or restaurant on Yelp, or even the funny cat video on YouTube.

Many describe the Internet as the global square or meeting place where the world can gather to discuss any topic at any time on any day of the year. It does not matter if the subject is popular, such as an election, or completely obscure like maple syrup–pouring techniques. The point is that the Internet allows for each and every person who has access to engage in the free exchange of ideas, assorted media, information, and knowledge. That makes it an incredibly powerful tool.

As Americans are now invested in watching streaming video, companies are looking at ways to monetize this and other facets of the Internet even more. This results in potential innovation being hindered by companies who want to treat each user differently. The same applies for matters of free speech on the Internet. Free speech should be just that. No company or organization should have the power to limit speech, online or offline, because someone might view it as offensive. Of course, there is the exception when someone threatens violence or to harm themselves; this absolutely demands that society take action to prevent it for the good of all. However, speech that is offensive to one might not be offensive to the other. It is just like burning an American flag; it might be utterly repulsive, but it is protected under the First Amendment of the United States Constitution.

Chapter 9
Ask first, shoot later

New York City in the 1980s and early 1990s was an interesting place to grow up. I loved the culture, excitement and constant bustle of a city always in motion. The streets were far from safe, but there was a character that made it feel like it was a living and breathing thing. But with all the good going on in New York City, there was also bad. The city was a dangerous place with dangerous people. It had earned the reputation of being a place where you could be robbed, raped, or murdered while just walking down the street. Not exactly a slogan that the tourism bureau wanted to promote. "Come to New York where the stabbings are part of the experience!"

In grade school my teachers began to provide me with the lessons that would prepare me for the world: reading, writing, and how to behave during a mugging. We were taught to not resist, look down at our own feet, and turn over our wallets to our assailants. When we saw an opening, we were to run to the nearest police officer or authority figure we could find. Of course, we chuckled and at recess played games of mugging. Then, things began to get serious. One of my classmates was mugged and returned to school the next day as an attraction. We peppered him with questions as he became a celebrity for having his wallet stolen while walking home from school. It gave that classmate an increased social standing in my class. Then, it happened to another student and another. Our curiosity gave way to a realization that we lived in a dangerous city. For some reason, I was never mugged and it still felt remotely distant.

My world was changed one day in late 1993 when I was getting off the school bus on my street corner. It was around 4:30 p.m. and dark, as the days were getting shorter and the nights longer. A large and unkempt man reached for my arm saying, "Hey! Yo, kid come here. I got a gun." Fear instantly shot through my body as a cold shiver ran down my spine. My legs tensed, my head turned to see there was nobody else around us, and instinct kicked in. I began sprinting toward my home. The run was about one hundred feet, but took what felt like forever. I vividly remember how I turned my head to see if this man was chasing me. I saw him standing where he had first accosted me, but he was turning toward me and reaching in his pocket. I made it into my apartment building and immediately told my mom what had happened. She hugged me and told me that everything would be all right and that I was safe.

That was the moment when my childhood ended and the realization hit me that this great city that I lived in was violent and dangerous. I was eleven years old. Fear overtook me, as I began begging my parents to pick me up from where the school bus would drop me off. I secretly carried a tiny key chain with a Swiss army knife in my backpack, thinking that I would use its tiny blade to keep me safe if I ever got into trouble again. I really wished that my knife were a gun, as if that was how I would ensure my own safety.

There is a constant battle in the American political world over the right to bear arms. Each and every time there is a mass shooting, both sides of the debate reflexively start shouting their views about guns and how the other side is out of touch. Second Amendment advocates know that at each instance of gun violence, anti-gun groups will seek to exploit that particular tragedy. They push for increased nationwide blanket regulations to curb what they see as an epidemic of gun violence.

To hear pro-gun control movement members tell it, guns are the greatest threat to national security that there is. We are living in a lawless and dangerous society where danger is lurking around every corner. To many, the frequent news of shootings across the country is too much to tolerate—they are correct in that we should not tolerate shootings—and must be stopped at all costs. These pro-gun control people mistakenly believe that more people are dying from gun-related homicides than over twenty years ago. The reality is that they are largely unaware that not only is overall crime down in the United States, but gun deaths have dropped 49 percent since 1993.

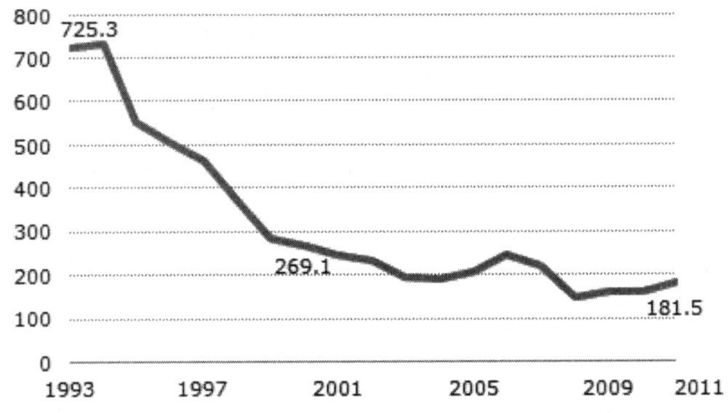

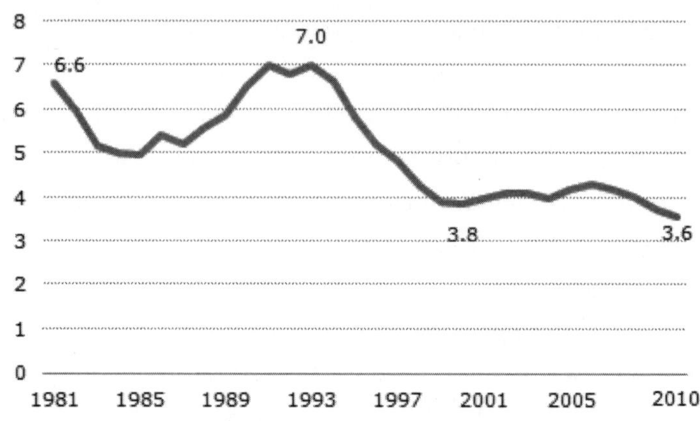

What is the cause of this mistaken belief? The rise of the twenty-four-hour cable news networks, as well as social media, has brought increased attention to any and all tragedies. News networks face a unique problem: they have to find watchable content to put on air 24/7. So, whenever there is a mass shooting, the media will run with the story and provide wall-to-wall coverage that saturates the American consciousness. No wonder anti-gun advocates feel that we are a nation under siege and at constant risk.

Let's look at the mass shootings that have happened since Columbine in 1999:

- April 20, 1999, Columbine, Colorado, thirteen dead, twenty-four wounded
- July 9, 1999, Atlanta, Georgia, nine dead, twelve wounded
- September 15, 1999, Fort Worth, Texas, seven dead, seven wounded

- November 2, 1999, Honolulu, Hawaii, seven dead
- December 26, 2000, Wakefield, Massachusetts, seven dead
- March 5, 2001, Santee, California, two dead, thirteen wounded
- July 8, 2003, Meridian, Mississippi, five dead, nine wounded
- March 21, 2005, Red Lake Indian Reservation, Minnesota, nine dead, seven wounded
- January 30, 2006, Goleta, California, six dead
- October 2, 2006, Nickel Mines, Pennsylvania, five dead, five wounded
- February 12, 2007, Salt Lake City, Utah, five dead, four wounded
- April 16, 2007, Blacksburg, Virginia, thirty-two dead, seventeen wounded
- December 5, 2007, Omaha, Nebraska, eight dead, four wounded
- February 14, 2008, Dekalb, Illinois, five dead, sixteen wounded
- April 3, 2009, Binghamton, New York, thirteen dead, four wounded
- November 5, 2009, Fort Hood, Texas, thirteen dead, thirty-two wounded
- August 3, 2010, Manchester, Connecticut, eight dead, two wounded
- January 8, 2011, Tucson, Arizona, six dead, eleven wounded
- October 12, 2011, Seal Beach, California, eight dead, one wounded
- April 2, 2012, Oakland, California, seven dead, three wounded
- July 20, 2012, Aurora, Colorado, twelve dead, fifty-eight wounded
- August 5, 2012, Oak Creek, Wisconsin, six dead, three wounded
- September 28, 2012, Minneapolis, Minnesota, six dead, two wounded
- December 14, 2012, Newtown, Connecticut, twenty-seven dead, one wounded
- June 7, 2013, Santa Monica, California, five dead
- September 16, 2013, Washington, DC, twelve dead, three wounded

- April 2, 2014, Fort Hood, Texas, three dead, sixteen wounded
- May 23, 2014, Isla Vista, California, six dead, seven wounded
- June 18, 2015, Charleston, South Carolina, nine dead
- July 16, 2015, Chattanooga, Tennessee, five dead, three wounded
- October 1, 2015, Roseburg, Oregon, nine dead, nine wounded
- November 29, 2015, Colorado Springs, Colorado, three dead, nine wounded
- December 2, 2015, San Bernardino, California, fourteen dead, twenty-one wounded

Each and every one of these shootings is a tragedy. They are a shock to the system. From Columbine on, 292 people have died in mass shootings in America. That is less than twenty people on average per year for fifteen years. During the same fifteen years, 303 people have been wounded in mass shootings in America since Columbine, just over twenty people a year. Even one dead or wounded a year is too many, but what other industry is targeted in such a way?

In 2013, gun deaths were just behind automobile deaths. According to the Center for Disease Control, there were 33,636 gun deaths in 2013 and 33,804 automobile deaths. In 2013, cars killed more Americans than firearms. Yet, there are no calls to ban or increase regulation of cars. In fact, many people just shrug it off and take the attitude that there is an inherent risk of death or injury with automobiles. If ever there were a time for a rational person to say, "Wait a second here . . ."

Pro-Second Amendment groups often cite this "automobiles versus guns" statistic and disconnect among the American people. Why shouldn't they? It's a legitimate point to raise and one in which the opposition has found it difficult to respond to. However, certain gun rights groups are harming the gun rights movement by over-the-top rhetoric and antics.

The National Rifle Association (NRA) is a large gun rights advocacy organization with a membership roll in the millions. It has a size and scope that few organizations in Washington can match. They have a massive war chest and are willing to spend what it takes to win in each and every political battle. Yet, they have a tendency to go overboard with their political moves. After the Columbine shooting, the NRA had a dilemma. They were to have their long-planned annual convention in Denver, only a few miles away from the tragedy. It was to be a three-day affair complete with a gun show. Local leaders and residents, still raw from the deaths of thirteen people, asked that the National Rifle Association cancel the event. The NRA was defiant and decided to go ahead with the convention, albeit modified to take place over one day instead of three. Officials, speakers, and attendees all emphasized that the National Rifle Association was not responsible for the actions of the shooters at the Columbine massacre. They were correct, but going ahead with the gathering had negative consequences for the gun rights movement.

From a public opinion standpoint, the National Rifle Association was being cold and insensitive toward the victims of Columbine. People across the nation could not believe that a constitutional rights organization was seemingly unconcerned with the pain of a community and nation that had been rocked to its core by an ugly act of pure evil. Worse still, it came off to many that the NRA was dancing on the graves of the dead . . . dead children. The optics of this were terrible and instantly nullified each legitimate point that gun rights advocates had to say. Suddenly, to the public, the NRA was callous and unfeeling. They were irrational in their love for guns and cared about them more than saving the lives of children. Not one bit of this was true, but nonetheless, the left had been given a gift that would keep on giving.

Instead of learning from their mistakes, the National Rifle Association continued down a path of harming the gun rights movement. They made it harder and harder for Second Amendment advocates to persuade Americans that guns were not the enemy. Essentially, the NRA was making some pretty large self-inflicted wounds. To urban and inner-city Americans, the NRA was neither popular nor a rational organization. They certainly were not helping to reduce the crime and gun violence within cities such as Chicago, Los Angeles, and New York.

By 1993, New York City, the crown jewel of America, had become the Rotting Apple. Rudolph William Louis Giuliani, a former United States attorney and high-ranking official in the Justice Department of President Reagan, was running for mayor as a Republican because New Yorkers were fed up with a city that was ungovernable and crime ridden. Democratic Mayor David Dinkins, who was in his first term at the helm of New York City and hoping to secure a second, presided over a city in turmoil. Under his watch, there had been riots—which took the city three days to respond to—increased crime, an out-of-control criminal element, and unemployment topping 11 percent. Giuliani based his campaign around a simple premise: New Yorkers need not live in fear.

Appealing to urban Democrats, Giuliani was elected the 107th Mayor of the City of New York on November 2, 1993. Winning by just over fifty thousand votes, he was the first Republican elected to the office in nearly thirty years. The last Republican elected was John Lindsay, who won in 1965. Immediately, Giuliani set out to save New York City from the abyss. New Yorkers, a breed of Americans that demands results like no other, would give no honeymoon to the tough-talking former prosecutor. They wanted to see action and they absolutely got it.

Mayor Giuliani took office and revolutionized how a big city is governed. To quell the tide of major crime and murders, he instituted a conservative principle known as Broken Windows, from a policy paper published in November 1982 in the *Atlantic* and authored by James Q. Wilson and George L. Kelling. They put forth a simple theory: if you strictly police and prosecute small crimes, you will prevent major crimes. Wilson and Kelling viewed minor crimes as a gateway to bigger criminal acts.

Another way in which Giuliani revolutionized governance of a city is through his implementation of COMPSTAT (shorthand for computer statistics). COMPSTAT was designed to hold the New York Police Department accountable from the top right down to the local precincts. They were able to track weekly crime statistics in a thorough and highly detailed manner. Now, crime could be mapped and resources could be deployed to take on whatever problem ailed a neighborhood.

Mayor Giuliani also decided to confront other factors that contributed to increased crime and decreased economic opportunity. He undertook initiatives that improved neighborhoods, reduced poverty, and increased opportunity.

Times Square was a haven for drugs, prostitution, and crime. The seedy underbelly it had become was the living embodiment of the New York City that had been rejected by voters in 1993. Giuliani set out to remake it. The police began enforcing the laws. No longer would Times Square be an area where self-moderated lawlessness was accepted. Yet, this was just one step to fixing the larger problem of Times Square. The businesses that were already in the neighborhood were less than family-friendly, as sex shops dominated the landscape. Through sheer force of will (and economic incentives), Giuliani convinced the most family-friendly brand there is to establish a store in Times Square. The Walt Disney Company opened a Disney Store on Forty-Second Street. This move paved the way for other stores to take up residence there. As Times Square transformed, so too did all of New York City. Unemployment and crime plummeted while opportunity skyrocketed.

The work of Rudy Giuliani in New York City was soon emulated and implemented across the country. Police departments and local governments saw the Giuliani approach as the gold standard of governing and crime fighting. Soon, Chicago, Denver, Los Angeles, Baltimore, Miami, Atlanta, New Orleans, and many more cities adopted Giuliani's policing model. It is no coincidence that the significant drop in crime across the United States from 1993 on is due to the innovation (and subsequent replication by other municipalities) of Rudy Giuliani.

One important factor in the crime reduction was not economic, but pragmatic. Strict enforcement of gun laws made New York City a safer place. Mayor Giuliani pushed for common-sense gun laws that kept New Yorkers safe. He pushed for the banning of assault weapons; allowing weapons of war to fall into the hands of criminals was not in the best interest of New Yorkers.

On a Sunday in 2007 on Fox News, Giuliani discussed his approach to guns and why he advocated to engage in the gun issue:

> I'm a strict constructionist, or I try to be. The Second Amendment is about as clear as it can be. It gives people the individual right to bear arms. I agree with that. I think that is a correct interpretation. That means that any restrictions have to be reasonable. And those restrictions largely have to do with criminal background, background of mental illness, and they should basically be done on the state-by-state level.[56]

Mayor Giuliani recognized the reality that Americans must be permitted to own a gun, which is outlined in the Second Amendment. He also recognized that conservatism is about empowering localities to make decisions, not an overbearing central government.

Mayors of other large cities joined Giuliani's effort to keep guns out of the hands of criminals. The National Rifle Association, on the other hand, did not. The NRA attacked Giuliani and the other big-city mayors. They did as much as they could to oppose New York's desire to reduce crime.

Millennials are generally more supportive of gun rights than the rest of the population. However, they also support more sensible

Large Majorities in Gun-Owning Households Favor Background Checks, Ban on Guns for Mentally Ill

% who favor each policy proposal

	Ban on assault weapons	Federal database of gun sales	Laws barring mentally ill from buying guns	Background checks for gun shows
	%	%	%	%
Total	57	70	79	85
Men	48	66	79	83
Women	65	74	79	87
White	58	66	86	89
Black	60	82	75	80
Hispanic	47	76	58	77
18-29	49	76	81	84
30-49	55	74	79	88
50-64	61	67	80	86
65+	63	61	75	82
Post-grad	72	77	91	92
College grad	66	67	87	89
Some college	58	71	85	87
HS or less	48	68	68	80
Community type				
Urban	62	78	76	86
Suburban	56	65	81	85
Rural	48	65	80	84
Gun in household (39% of total)	49	61	84	87
No gun in household (58% of total)	64	78	76	85

Survey conducted July 14-20, 2015. Whites and blacks include only non-Hispanics; Hispanics can be of any race.

PEW RESEARCH CENTER

gun laws such as barring the mentally ill from owning a gun and background checks for people buying weapons at gun shows.

Urban residents also want these laws in order to protect themselves and their families. Urban Republicans should embrace these numbers and support sensible gun protections while still supporting the Second Amendment. This can be achieved by having states and local governments set their own gun laws. Cities such as New York, Chicago, and Los Angeles need stricter gun laws in order to provide adequate safety for their citizens. Again, this is another instance where what works in New York City certainly will not work in Boise, Idaho. This position will be mocked by the left, who will reflexively attack it as being insensitive. Let them. It will show their only response to serious positions taken by Republicans is that they engage in hyperventilation.

For some, such as Republicans in New York, Los Angeles, and Chicago, they should make it a personal goal for the National Rifle Association to oppose them. It only furthers support for the Republican in the urban area. Each and every time that they are questioned about this, the response should be the same, "We are given a choice between making sure the mentally ill don't get guns or a tragic alternative."

Yes, that is an extreme thing to say, as it does not remotely capture the complexity of the situation. However, it does resonate with urban residents and millennials.

At the same time, we can further explain the position of urban Republicans as one that is consistent with our conservative and federalist values. The decisions about regulating who has access to guns are best left up to the state and local governments, not some central authority in disconnected Washington, DC.

Anti-gun advocates often use the argument that the Constitution is a living, breathing document that evolves with the times. They point out that at the time it was authored, the United States was fresh off a revolution that saw ordinary citizens defeat the world's leading army. They didn't do so with pitchforks, but with their own muskets. There was the threat of invasion from foreign powers, as America was an incredibly new country and a far cry from the superpower that it is today. They even concede that raids by native tribes were a danger. And then, anti-gun advocates contrast that situation with today's circumstances. They stress that we do not face the threat of an invading army—sorry Canada, but the thought of you invading the United States is far funnier than it is serious. They say that had the Founding Fathers known that guns would evolve to be able to fire multiple rounds in a matter of seconds (i.e., not be loaded via ramrod such as a musket and take over a minute to load a single shot), they would not have even bothered to include the Second Amendment—that's completely farcical. Anti-gun proponents then commit their fatal error and push the narrative that we no longer need to fear an overbearing central government that is removed from the reality of what is going on in the country, as well as the beliefs of the people.

Our founding fathers revolted against the same type of government that anti-gun champions claim do not exist. They are clearly oblivious to the irony here. Should they get their way and ban all guns, they are making the federal government into an overbearing central government by having it control the actions of its citizens from the bubble of Washington, DC. Additionally, that federal government would be disconnected from the reality of its citizens' beliefs. Remember, the majority of the United States believes in the Second Amendment. This belief does not mean that Americans feel it should be permissible for a person to walk into a store and buy a gun as easily as they buy a candy bar. What United States citizens do believe is that Americans should have the ability to buy a firearm or gun provided they go through a sensible and rational process.

Chapter 10
Bordering on insanity

Growing up, I quickly came to realize that I had a unique identity. My dad was Jewish and my mom Protestant. My mom could trace part of her family all the way back to the *Mayflower*, while my dad could go back a century to when his paternal grandfather, Isidore Siegfried, came to the United States. In 1904, Isidore took the same journey as many immigrants; he sailed across the sea and into New York Harbor, past the Statue of Liberty, and landed on Ellis Island. He began his life as a new American citizen working a pushcart in New York City. Within a few years, he had pulled himself up by his bootstraps and was the owner of his own department store, the Beehive. Not bad for a European Jew lacking an education.

On my mom's side of the family, she was the child of an even more recent immigrant. My grandfather, Hugh Goodman, was born in Scotland and immigrated to the United States after serving in the British Royal Navy in World War II. He became a successful advertising executive and had a tremendous love of his adopted country. My grandfather was a staunch Republican and never voted for a Democrat in his entire life (save once suffering a lapse in judgment and backing Adlai Stevenson in one of his two races against Dwight D. Eisenhower). However, he felt that one was not a true American until having eaten one hundred pieces of apple pie and having attended one hundred New York Yankees games. He might have been onto something that we should consider adopting.

Isidore Siegfried and Hugh Goodman were both a part of the fabric of America. They had their own unique experiences and backgrounds that made the United States a country filled with rich diversity. They each came to the United States and lived their own American story. It is why I am proud of my heritage and celebrate it. Additionally, it serves as a reminder that the United States is a nation of immigrants whose fabric is woven with millions upon millions of unique American stories. Each and every immigrant should be celebrated, as they bring their own unique contribution to the country and to our national heritage. We owe it to them to reform our immigration system.

In January 2016, the Pew Research Center released a study that almost half of Hispanic voters are millennials. A record 27.3 million Hispanic Americans will be eligible to cast their votes in the 2016 presidential election, with 44 percent of them being millennials (twelve million). The growth of this demographic is largely attributed to youth and Hispanic immigrants becoming United States citizens. They are very interested in the issue of immigration and will judge candidates accordingly.

The immigration process in America is broken. There is no debate about that fact from either side of the aisle. Each group recognizes that we must revise and reform our immigration system. The borders are porous, the screening process is heavily flawed, and we have an ineffectual bureaucracy overseeing the whole thing. However, what Democrats and Republicans differ on is the answer to the question of what to do.

Democrats, under the guise of moral obligation, believe that we should provide citizenship to as many immigrants as possible, as they will be future voters. Why shouldn't they? It's in their best interest to try to expand the number of people who vote for them. Yet, Democrats do so at the expense of the existing laws and financial security of the nation (and that doesn't even cover the national security risk of the recent influx of immigrants and refugees that have been involved in terrorist activities).

Let's face it; passing meaningful legislation in Congress is becoming increasingly less common. Each side will dig in and take inflexible positions without being willing to compromise. So, Democrats have resorted to the tactics of ignoring the laws that are on the books while trying to provide backdoor citizenship.

Democrats have created what are known as "sanctuary cities," places that have implemented policies of not enforcing federal immigration law when it comes to illegal immigrants and undocumented workers. This stance is due to either local laws that explicitly state that the local government will not comply with federal immigration laws and detention requests, or a de facto policy of not enforcing the laws on the books. This behavior has led to serious consequences.

On July 1, 2015, Kate Steinle was walking on a pier in San Francisco with her father when a gun went off. She fell to the ground, having been struck in the chest by a bullet, and was pronounced dead two hours later. Kate Steinle was thirty-two years old. The shooter was Juan Francisco Lopez-Sanchez, an undocumented worker who had been deported from the United States back to his native Mexico five times.[57] He was in the custody of San Francisco authorities in April 2015, but was released after charges of marijuana possession were dropped. Lopez-Sanchez was released from custody despite federal authorities having a standing detention order on file against him. San Francisco authorities chose to ignore it because their leaders did not like the federal immigration laws.

Predictably, Steinle's family filed a federal lawsuit against the sheriff of San Francisco for failing to detain and transfer Sanchez to federal law enforcement authorities.[58] One would think that this tragedy would cause San Francisco and other Democrat-controlled cities to reconsider their sanctuary city policy. Nope, they did not. In fact, San Francisco's mayor and board of supervisors, all Democrats, used the increased media attention to reaffirm their commitment to a sanctuary city policy. On October 20, 2015, the San Francisco Board of Supervisors voted unanimously on a resolution that stated they support the sheriff not cooperating with federal immigration and law enforcement agencies.[59]It disgustingly and needlessly turned the death of an innocent American woman into a political hot potato.

The death of Kate Steinle is the most vivid example of how Democrats and their policy of not enforcing the laws they do not like, not only endanger our own ability to govern, but put our very citizens at risk. Instead of enforcing the laws that are on the books to reduce illegal immigration, Democrats seek to incentivize illegal behavior on the part of undocumented workers.

In 2015, we saw proposals for illegal immigrants to be granted Obamacare, free college tuition, and other government services. In New York City, 2015 was the year that undocumented immigrants were allowed to receive city government-issued identification cards without fear of being reported to any law enforcement agency, be it federal or local. What was the logic for issuing all of these handouts? Offering such government benefits would enable the left to make the case that since the government already gives illegal immigrants the same services and benefits of ordinary citizens, then we should just formally declare them citizens. (Of course, they will thank Democrats at the ballot box when they attain citizenship and the right to vote.) In 2016, the New York City Council is now bringing up legislation that would give illegal immigrants the right to vote in New York City elections.[60]

Such a proposal being enacted would be a disaster for the Republican Party in New York City. They are already a marginalized sector of the population and Republicans have been talking about how they should follow the law. Our desire to see our immigration laws that are on the books being enforced naturally and properly puts us at odds with undocumented workers and their families. How willing would they be to vote for any Republican if they were given the right to vote? What illegal immigrant would vote for a candidate that believes that they are engaging in criminal activity and should be punished for doing so?

These various proposals are just not proper and are counter to the laws that are on the books. Not only are such attempts at back-door citizenship for illegals unfair to legal immigrants that are on a legal path to citizenship; it incentivizes illegal behavior. What immigrant would choose the longer and legal path to citizenship when they would be rewarded for taking the illegal path to citizenship?!

Republicans, who are in the right for opposing the misguided and deficient Democratic immigration policy proposals, are quickly painted by the left and media as xenophobic and racist nativists. Somehow, we conservatives are portrayed as hating Mexicans and Hispanics because we have legitimate reasons to oppose the Democratic orthodoxy. Instead of challenging Republicans and their policy proposals with an honest intellectual debate, Democrats and the media counter by slinging mud.

The reality is that immigrants to the United States come from all different countries and parts of the world. They are Mexican, Ecuadorian, Brazilian, Canadian, French, English, Chinese, Japanese, and even Finnish. However, about half of all immigrants to the United States from 1965 on are from Latin America. This enables the left's mendacious argument to be made in broad brush-strokes: Republicans are anti-Latino. Nobody accuses us of being anti-Finland or anti-Canada.

Immigrant Share of Population

Percent of U.S. population that is foreign born

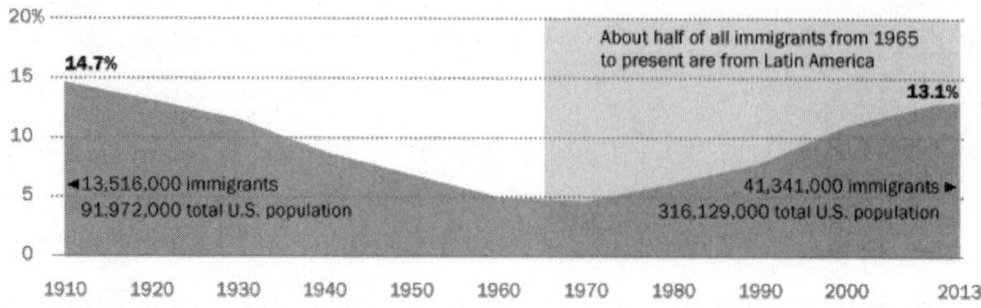

Source: U.S. Census Bureau, "Historical Census Statistics on the Foreign-Born Population of the United States: 1850-2000" and Pew Research Center tabulations of 2010 and 2013 American Community Survey (IPUMS)

PEW RESEARCH CENTER

In just over one hundred years, we have seen the percentage of the United States population that is foreign-born drop from almost 15 percent in 1910 to under 5 percent in 1965, and then increase to 13.1 percent in 2013. The overall population and the population of foreign-born residents during that same hundred-year period more than tripled. In translation, foreign-born residents of the United States play a large part in the daily function of American society and progress. Chances are they either interact daily with at least one voter or, provided they have achieved citizenship status, they will have their own set of issues and views which they expect politicians to address. There is no reason for us to ignore these millions of potential voters.

It would be advantageous and morally proper for Republicans to seek the support and vote of these forty-one million residents. An initial step toward this goal is to help these people become full-fledged citizens. No, this does not mean giving American citizenship to people who are in the country illegally. Breaking the law is not something that deserves reward or encouragement (although there is the complex problem of what to do with their children).

Almost every single weekday, thousands of people walk into a United States federal courthouse as aliens, and a few hours later reemerge as American citizens. This is the completion of the long and arduous process of becoming a United States citizen. Many of these newest Americans walk out of that federal courthouse with tears in their eyes. It is an emotional and almost spiritual moment. The long and hard journey that they have traveled to become an American is now complete. They have become a part of the greatest nation on earth with all of the rights afforded to its citizens. These daily ceremonies where a federal judge administers the oath of citizenship to a cross section of the world that has played by the rules are to be cherished and celebrated. Let's acknowledge this special process by encouraging those that adhere to the law to become a part of the fabric of the United States while discouraging those who seek illegal shortcuts.

When Democrats start talking about anything that aids illegal immigrants, Republicans should not take the bait and respond to the premise of the question. Instead, we should adhere to the rule of answering the question that we wish we were asked and to focus on GOP programs that encourage and enable citizenship for the people that come to the United States seeking to become Americans by playing by the rules. There is no reason that Republicans should give the Democrats what they want: a debate over illegal immigrants. The pivot to this will allow us to move out from under the shadow that the left has cast on us. Charges of xenophobia, nativism, and racism will be null and void.

Democrats have benefited from the tone of the 2016 Republican presidential primary season. The loudest voices have all come out and taken positions that many view as anti-immigrant and bordering on racist. In his announcement speech, Donald Trump claimed that Mexico was sending criminals and rapists across the border and into the United States. Many took this to mean that Trump had called Mexicans criminals and rapists. Later, Trump responded to the shooting in San Bernardino by calling for halting of all Muslims from entering the United States. It didn't matter if they were here on vacation or trying to immigrate. To Trump, they were all to be banned. This December 2015 proposal earned swift condemnation from Republican leaders including Speaker of the House Paul Ryan and former Vice President Dick Cheney. Despite these condemnations, in the public's eye, the damage was already done. Republicans were xenophobic and racist people who did not like people with races and religions that were different from their own. Again, this is not even remotely true, but the left did their damnedest to portray Republicans as such.

Now, we must moderate our tone and show sympathy for the plight of immigrants and refugees. At the same time, Republicans need to vigorously attack and rebut any claims of xenophobia. First, it is important to acknowledge the fact that immigrants, both legal and illegal, contribute to our economy. This contribution is visible when you walk down a New York City street. The food deliveryman is scurrying with lunch or dinner from the restaurant where he works to the customer's apartment. These deliverymen are not highly paid and highly skilled workers. Rather, they are people willing to work a job with virtually no prospect of upward mobility and are barely compensated for the duties that they perform. The same goes for the dishwasher from Nigeria, the nanny from Jamaica, the housekeeper from Finland, etc. Such positions are far from desirable, but they do help these men and women not only pay the bills, but pursue their own American dream.

These legal immigrants are vital to the economic success of the United States. Were our immigration policies to become stricter and make it so that these positions would be filled with educated and skilled American labor, the consequences would be severe. These workers would demand higher pay and the prices of every good and service would skyrocket. This would, in turn, cause the overall cost of living to rise throughout the country. It's a recipe for a bad economy.

Not only are immigrants more willing to hold vital and lower-paying positions, they pay into the economy of the country and the places in which they live. Their paychecks have taxes deducted from them, and they file tax returns. Immigrants are not taking services from the government without paying for them. Their tax contributions are compensation for government services provided, including, but not limited to, police services, the protection of the fire department, the maintenance of infrastructure—you get the idea. Numerous studies have found that immigrants pay between $90 and $140 billion a year in federal, state, and local taxes. That's a lot of tax dollars.

Immigrants also do more than pay taxes and work jobs that few Americans want. They use their hard-earned money to contribute to the economy through commerce. They are consumers who buy goods and services. Immigrants want the new television, computer, and gaming system, not to mention the more essential goods like food, clothes, and personal care products. If they were to disappear from the United States due to stricter immigration policies, then the country's economy would suffer and Americans would lose their jobs as corporate profits dropped. Make no mistake; immigrants are vital to the United States economy.

Again, immigration is an issue that sets off passionate feelings on all sides of the issue. It is important that Republicans adhere to calm and rational methods of presenting our policy proposals on the matter. While doing this, Republicans should use this as an opportunity to highlight how the agenda of Democrats actually makes the immigration problem worse.

One thing that few, if any, are talking about is the issue of foreign-born workers and immigrants in the American labor force. In 2014, the Bureau of Labor Statistics reported that 25.7 million foreign-born workers were part of the United States labor force. That's 16.5 percent of the American labor force. The Bureau of Labor Statistics also found that Hispanics accounted for 48.3

percent of the foreign-born labor force in 2014 and Asians accounted for 24.1 percent. Again, these are ethnic groups that the GOP must recruit to win and can ill-afford to alienate. Foreign-born workers don't just work the jobs that Americans don't want to do, but they also take positions that require a high level of skills and expertise. This is something that should be openly discussed and utilized to push the Republican education plan.

Wait a second . . . How is education connected to the issue of immigration? It very much is, and it impacts it in a complex manner. The United States education system is ranked the fourteenth best quality education system in the world. Who is ahead of the United States? South Korea, Japan, Singapore, Hong Kong, Finland, United Kingdom, Canada, Netherlands, Ireland, Poland, Denmark, Germany, and Russia. Yes, Vladimir Putin's Russia is ahead of the United States in quality of education. These countries churn out well-educated graduates who want to work the best job possible. The United States, which is the most important country in the global economy, is an enticing place to live and work.

American companies seek to hire the best talent available for the positions they have open. Let's examine the hypothetical situation of General Electric having to decide between two candidates for a single position: director of digital marketing. One candidate, Tom, is American-educated, graduated from college with a 3.0 GPA, has held a few unremarkable internships, and says he is the person for the job. The other person applying for the position, Jyrki, was educated in Finland, attended Oxford University for both undergraduate and postgraduate studies focusing on digital marketing, had a 4.0 GPA, and has worked in the widgets industry for a few years. Which candidate would you choose? Clearly, the foreign-born candidate who went to Oxford is the clear choice for the job.

If the United States were to adopt our education agenda that was previously outlined in this book, we can and will close the education gap between the United States and other countries.

When this gap is closed (and hopefully the United States reclaims the mantle of the top country for education in the world), American companies will have a deeper talent pool of American workers from which to hire. Improving education in the United States will also improve our ability to innovate and be a boon to the economy. Better education enables better opportunities for Americans to be hired for American jobs.

Then there is the issue of what we do with the children of undocumented workers. Many illegal immigrants come across the border, find jobs, and assimilate into American society. They join a community and have a family. Their children, who are born in the United States, are automatically granted American citizenship under birthright citizenship. Some members of the Republican Party have called for ending this practice. Illegal immigrants believe that if they were to have a child in the United States, they would be able to stay because their son or daughter was an American citizen and the United States does not like to split up families. It is where the term "anchor baby" comes from, as these children literally anchor the undocumented immigrants to the United States.

Ending birthright citizenship is not the way to go. As Robert Tracinski wrote in the *Federalist*:

> Make no mistake, eliminating birthright citizenship would require an overthrow of established traditions. It implies a reckless urge to break down ancient legal principles without inquiring why those traditions existed in the first place. In short, it requires precisely the sort of thing conservatives are supposed to be against.[61]

Ending birthright citizenship is not in keeping with our values. As stated before, keeping in line with our principles is important when it is inconvenient. Some might view birthright citizenship as inconvenient to the party when it comes to illegal immigration, but it is accepted law and tradition. To end it would go against the very principles we, as conservatives, hold dear.

Parents who are illegal immigrants that have children in the United States should be given the ability to stay in the country with their kids. This should not be something that enhances their claims for American citizenship. Actually, it should prohibit them from becoming American citizens. Why not create a new visa program that allows parents to stay in the United States legally, but that does not allow them to pursue a path to citizenship without getting in the very back of the line? Deporting the parents would punish the child for a sin that they did not commit. It also would devastate the foundation of that particular family.

Urban areas are home to vibrant immigrant communities. New York City has Chinatown, Little Italy, Spanish Harlem/El Barrio, Brighton Beach, etc. There are numerous ethnic enclaves in New York City and other urban areas. Their residents were at one time immigrants (or their prior generations were), but have assimilated themselves to the United States. They love baseball, the Super Bowl, the Fourth of July, and apple pie. Illegal immigrants are part of these communities, too, and they contribute economically to the United States. The Manhattan Institute's Peter D. Salins wrote in the *New York Post*:

> Regarding their impact on the economy: for starters, for many American industries—and most American consumers—all immigrants, including illegal ones, have been a huge economic asset; countless studies show they not only don't take jobs away from American workers, they eagerly tackle ones that the native-born shun. Contrary to the popular canards, they save American taxpayers money because the payroll, sales, and other taxes they pay far exceed the cost of government services or payments they receive.[62]

There are other steps that we can take to improve our immigration system. What about strengthening E-Verify? It is the government service that allows employers to verify that the information provided by an employee on their Form I-9 matches government databases. It is done entirely by the Internet. E-Verify helps to cut down on fraudulent workers who claim that they are in the United States legally. Yet, this is entirely optional when it comes to employers. No business is required to use E-Verify; it is an entirely voluntary program. Making it mandatory for employers to ensure their employees are who they say they are will bolster our immigration system. It also will add another facet that would make illegal immigrants think twice before coming to the United States for work.

Another vital reform would be to finally implement the recommendation of the 9/11 Commission, a bipartisan group of officials and elder statesmen who investigated the September 11 attacks, that we have a biometric entry and exit tracking system. The recommendation was made in 2004. To this day, it has not been implemented. Roy Beck, the president of the immigration reform group NumbersUSA described exit tracking as:

> A biometric exit system is essential to deterring visa overstays effectively. It will help to eliminate errors that regularly occur when collecting and accessing biographic data, and will make identity fraud more difficult. It is easy to steal someone else's identity papers but not so their fingerprints. A biometric screening system will enhance and facilitate data-sharing, which will lead to better national security, while also helping to combat international terrorism.[63]

Beck goes further and explains that in December 2015, the State Department was forced to admit that not only had they admitted over 9,500 foreign nationals with terrorist connections into the United States, but that they had no idea of whether or not they had left the country or were still in the United States. The current immigration system literally has no way of verifying that a foreign national has left the country. It relies on the honor code.

Implementation of the biometric entry and exit system is already underway, but the problem is that the only aspect that has been established is the entry portion. The exit side of the biometric entry and exit program still does not exist. This creates a gap that terrorists can exploit. Remember, the 9/11 hijackers were in the United States on expired visas. The biometric entry and exit system might not have necessarily prevented the September 11 attacks, but it certainly would have put the attackers on the radar of law enforcement organizations and officials.

E-Verify and the biometric entry and exit system are in no way anti-immigrant. They, like all other Republican immigration proposals, help to not only protect the United States from criminal and nefarious activity, but to protect the many immigrants who enter the United States legally and abide by the laws. It does so by removing people who are trying to bypass the law of the land on immigration and thus jump ahead of legal immigrants who might be waiting to become naturalized citizens. Additionally, it removes competition for government services and makes the United States a safer place.

Our system is broken. Two refugees were arrested on charges of terrorism within a day of one another in January 2016. Yet, the screening process of refugees and immigrants has seen no reform despite repeated calls. Republicans have called for a fix to prevent terrorists from exploiting our goodwill toward immigrants, but they might as well be shouting into the wind, as Democrats see adding any stricter measures as a threat to expanding their own influence and popularity with minorities.

The 2016 presidential campaign saw Donald Trump push the idea that the United States needed to build a massive wall along the US border with Mexico and make the Mexican government pay for its construction and maintenance. Ted Cruz also promoted the building of the wall, but did not say that Mexico would bear financial responsibility. Many among the anti-illegal immigration crowd cheered this proposal. To them, it represented a literal physical barrier that would stop illegal aliens from making their way into the United States. However, it would not drastically reduce or impact the number of illegal immigrants already in the United States.

A "great wall," as Trump calls it, wouldn't fix a bigger problem of the immigration system. Forty percent of illegal immigrants entered the United States legally on valid visas.[64] Only, when it came time for them to leave, they never did. There was no incentive to do so, as US officials rarely, if at all, would pursue people who overstayed their visas. This is a major indicator that our immigration system is broken and is not enforcing the rules that are on the books. A wall does not stop a person from legally entering the country on a work, tourist, or student visa and never leaving. Our failure to track down people who overstay their visas has made it so that the simplest way to get into the country is to come in like everybody else and just never leave. It is much easier than trying to sneak across the border while battling the elements and evading the border patrol.

This problem would be readily solved should E-Verify be used. It would allow United States officials to have a better idea of the whereabouts of immigrants who overstay their visas. Then, they could track down and take action against those who choose to remain in the United States illegally. What would also help is if the people overseeing our immigration system would work to discourage and prevent visa overstays. Were they to crack the whip and do their jobs, 40 percent of illegal immigrants would not be due to aliens overstaying their visas.

The hostile tone toward immigrants received a large swath of coverage during the 2016 presidential campaign. It helped to tar the Republican Party as being composed of rabid xenophobes, which Republicans are not, but the desire to reform our broken immigration system combined with the loud anti-immigrant voices of a small sect of the GOP has helped make a case that the party really is overrun by nativists.

Let's end our pushes to kick out illegal immigrants by giving them a pathway to citizenship through legally immigrating into the United States. Let's end the practice of sanctuary cities. Let's stop demonizing and punishing the children of undocumented immigrants. Let's embrace the conservative policy of birthright citizenship. Let's secure our borders and make it harder for terrorists to exploit them. Doing so would create a more economically viable and safer America.

Chapter 11
A true safe space

NOT A DAY HAS GONE BY THAT I HAVE NOT THOUGHT ABOUT that beautiful fall day. I was in the final year of high school at a boarding school in Maine, sitting in geology class when I became anxious for no explainable reason. The bell rang to signal it was the end of second period and I joined my classmates in the march across campus to our daily all-school meeting. As we filed into the meeting room while waiting for the morning meeting to begin, the assistant director of admissions pulled me aside.

"Doesn't your dad work in the World Trade Center?" she asked with a smile.

"No. His office is in midtown Manhattan. Why do you ask?"

"Oh, a plane crashed into it," she casually said. From the way she said it, so carefree and airy, I was a bit perplexed as to why she even bothered to ask.

I walked toward a teacher of mine that I had a class with later. What I was going to talk to him about—I cannot remember. I looked up to see my advisor, Matt Crane, standing near the door. It was odd, as he never attended these school events. I sat down next to my teacher and faced the center of the room where the headmaster,

Rist Bonnefond, was standing, his face was red and he was visibly upset.

"Well, looks like Mr. Bonnefond just had to expel somebody," I said to the teacher. "Any idea who it is?"

"None," came my teacher's reply.

Then I turned to the weird plane crash question I had just received and was still trying to process. "Hey, did you hear about that plane hitting the World Trade Center? That pilot has to be an idiot and eligible for a Darwin Award."

The teacher chuckled and said, "No, I didn't. What was it? Single-engine prop plane? That pilot couldn't have been very good if he flew into the World Trade Center."

The morning meeting began and Mr. Bonnefond began with his traditional greeting. "Good morning!" he said, but this time lacking its usual charm, enthusiasm, and drawn-out playfulness. "It is my responsibility to share with you some terrible news . . ."

The rest of the day was a blur. I can only remember bits and pieces. I remember that my advisor, Mr. Crane, had immediately walked me to his house so that I could get to a television. I was in shock and still trying to rationalize what I had been told by the assistant admissions director when I had first walked into the meeting room. There was no way what we had been told by Mr. Bonnefond was true. It had to be a misunderstanding and just some idiot in a prop plane being a terrible pilot.

Then, I saw it on television. One tower had a giant gaping hole in it, from which smoke was pouring out. The other tower . . . it wasn't there. It didn't make sense.

I spent about twenty minutes at Mr. Crane's house, attempting to reach my family on the phone and to wrap my mind around what was going on. It just didn't feel right not to be with them in this moment. Unsuccessful, I walked back to my dorm.

Entering my dorm's common room, where our TV and couches were, everybody was quiet with mouths agape. The screen showed just a cloud of dust and smoke. It didn't make sense. Without even having to be asked, a friend turned to me and said, "The second tower . . . it just collapsed." Twenty guys and I who were in the final year of high school and preparing to go to college just stayed where we were for the next ninety minutes. The only noises that one could hear—aside from the sound of the anchor on the television—were the gasps of friends and palms patting the backs of others. Not one of us knew what to do to comfort one another. We just did what we did after we lost a soccer or hockey game: clapped one another on the back while shaking our heads.

September 11, 2001, was one of the most beautiful days that I had ever seen on my school's campus, which only added to the utterly surreal feeling that day had.

The days and weeks afterward were strange for me. My mind understood what had happened, but a part of me just could not comprehend it. My family was all safe and unharmed, so when the opportunity came for me to go home for a long weekend in October 2001, I uncharacteristically opted not to. I didn't finally go home until Thanksgiving.

The day after Thanksgiving, I met my parents at New York's City Hall. My dad had arranged for us to receive a private tour of Ground Zero, and we were to be taken there from city hall in a golf cart. The journey to this sacred ground was surreal. Here we were, moving at five miles per hour down Broadway in a golf cart.

The first thing I noticed was the air. Despite being blocks away from Ground Zero, my eyes burned and I could taste the dust in my mouth. It is one of those sensations that are impossible to forget. To this day, I can still feel my eyes burning.

As we entered Ground Zero, there were men in white plastic coveralls holding water cannons and spraying the wheels of every vehicle that entered or left. My guide explained that they did not want contaminants to enter or leave the quarantine area. The stark reality of what had happened began to finally sink in.

The most striking part of this visit to Ground Zero was seeing the destruction. The sheer scope of the devastation was impossible to fully realize on television. Actually seeing it underscored the true horror of the terrorist attack.

While standing on a visitor's platform that had been constructed so that dignitaries and families of victims could view what was left of the World Trade Center, a police officer approached me. He could see that I was attempting to grapple with what had happened. He told me how the site, over two months since those dreadful attacks, was still on fire underground. It was stunning and baffling to think that this was possible.

Those two days were my unique experience with September 11. Many millennials that are old enough to remember 9/11, of which there are few, can remember where they were on that fateful day. It helped to shape my own view that we must do everything in our power to prevent threats from being able to take any action that would harm the United States or its citizens. For each and every older millennial, it was both a unique and shared experience that signaled the end of their innocence and start of life in the real world.

New Yorkers were also particularly impacted by the attacks of September 11. The days following the horrifying tragedy demonstrated the strength and goodness of New Yorkers and Americans throughout the country. The phrase "Never Forget" took hold of the national consciousness. We would never forget the people who perished on that day. We would never forget the firefighters, police officers, and other first responders who rushed to the World Trade Center and Ground Zero to save as many as possible. We would never forget the Americans who sacrificed themselves on United Airlines Flight 93 to prevent another target being struck. We would never forget the lessons of that fateful day.

Urban residents, particularly New Yorkers, have not forgotten about September 11. It is a part of them. It colors and influences their opinions on life. Our own unique and shared experience of 9/11 has made us more aware of the dangers of the real world. We know that threats exist and that the world is not a place of perfect harmony. We prefer not to fight, but we will when the situation requires—for we can never repeat what happened that September morning. We must never forget, even when other events encroach and shape how the country views America's involvement in world affairs.

The majority of millennials actually came of age during the Iraq War. They watched the United States invade in 2003 and then struggle to keep the peace as Iraq descended into chaos. The news out of post-war Iraq was not good for several years. Sectarian violence saw many men, women, and children dying every single day. There were also the increased casualties among American soldiers who were being wounded and killed by insurgent fighters.

These insurgents didn't play by normal rules. They used guerilla tactics and sought to instill the fear that they could strike any place at any time. Their preferred method of attack was using improvised explosive devices (IEDs) that they would leave on the side of the road or in a public place. When American soldiers would get close, a terrorist spotter that was hidden would detonate the bomb. Soon, there were regular reports of wounded soldiers who had been injured, maimed, or worse. It had a chilling effect on the psyche of the American people and really shaped the foreign policy views of millennials. Now, millennials are rather reluctant to use military force when it involves committing troops to the fight, a.k.a. "boots on the ground."

It does not help matters that when compared to other generations, millennials believe the world is not as threatening to the United States or to other nations. There is this belief that if the United States were to "stay in its lane" and not interfere with others, then the number of external threats would be minimal. It is a live-and-let-live approach that is based on the way they want to see the world as opposed to how the world actually is.

For all the talk about safe spaces by protesters, no space is truly safe unless it is protected from external threats. As some are jumping up and down protesting the microaggressions of college administrations, there are those who are actively planning *macroaggressions* against them and the United States.

Today, the United States faces threats from terrorist organizations including ISIS and Al Qaeda. On top of that, there are state actors who are threatening national security and stability. Russia, North Korea, Iran, and others seek to exert their authority in their spheres of influence, in addition to working toward diminishing the stature of the United States of America.

Don't believe that terrorism is a threat to the United States? In 2015, the United States faced the most Islamic terrorist plots within the country since September 11. The total number of Islamic terrorist plots in the United States was thirteen.[65] Sure, that seems like a small number, but it is not. This "small number" is actually more than the total number of plots in the years 2012, 2013, and 2014 combined. With the rise of ISIS since 2014, as well as the increase in homegrown Islamic terrorism, the United States will face even more potential attacks in the years to come.

Democrats, led by the ineffectual President Barack Obama, have failed to recognize the danger that ISIS poses to the United States. In December 2015, the San Bernardino shooting was carried out by a couple who had pledged their allegiance to ISIS. In January 2016, a man shot a Philadelphia police officer and later told investigators that he did so in the name of ISIS. These were clear signals that the threat of ISIS had made it to our shores. What did the Obama administration do in response? They called poverty and climate change the root cause of terrorism and then used the shootings as an excuse to implement stricter gun control through executive action. No matter where one comes down on the issue of guns, there is no denying that Obama's move has nothing to do with terrorism. His executive order is a bit like a doctor saying the way he is going to cure a broken hand is by amputating it.

In truth, there were warning signs that ISIS was going to be a threat to the United States homeland. In the summer of 2014, a man attacked several New York City police officers with a hatchet. The attack severely injured one officer. The attacker was killed by the NYPD at the scene of the terrorist attack. The director of the

FBI concluded a month later that this was indeed a terrorist attack and that the perpetrator had been inspired by ISIS.

The response of Democrats? Yawns.

After the attacks on Paris in November of 2015, President Obama insisted that we should stay the course in our strategy for dealing with ISIS. Hillary Clinton echoed this sentiment. Republicans and the rest of America collectively said, "What?!"

Republicans have called for taking the fight to ISIS, including putting "boots on the ground" so that we can end this threat once and for all. Yet, the appetite of millennials to use military force is not there. A 2011 Pew Research Center study found that nearly two-thirds of millennials believe that using military force to resolve a problem like terrorism only leads to further hatred of the United States and creates more terrorism.[66] It is a vicious cycle in their minds. Millennials prefer multilateralism and diplomacy.

A millennial, Aaron Strickland of the Heritage Foundation, wrote in the *Daily Signal* that millennials need to understand what exactly American power has enabled to happen:

> Millennials must understand that America has utilized its status as a dominant global power to ensure freedom of commerce and travel around the globe (and in space). The world economic system we see today is no accident—it was created through a strong American global presence. The reduction of American leadership throughout the world could result in the restriction of these freedoms.
>
> The goals and dreams of millennials are not at all different from generation X or the baby boomers in that they desire a nation that is economically strong and fiscally responsible—one that champions the right to life, liberty, and property for all individuals, and a nation that champions peace throughout the world. Therefore, they must understand that the key to ensuring that these diplomatic and economic

> goals are met is to have an effective and efficient military force.[67]

Strickland fully understands the problems of this dangerous world in which we live. Yet, two-thirds of millennials feel that his rational approach is not in our national best interest. So how do we straddle both a policy of using military force and a policy that emphasizes diplomacy? These two approaches seem to be diametrically opposed to one another. Many believe that they are black and white issues, but they actually are issues that complement one another.

Much like the carrot and the stick, we can see that diplomacy is aided by military force and vice versa. Today, there exists a golden opportunity for the United States to strengthen its hand in the world, make it a safer place, and show millennials that we can use both force and diplomacy to achieve our objectives without suffering blowback. That opportunity is with the nation of North Korea.

North Korea exists as a state to fulfill one purpose: maintaining the grip of power of its leader, Kim Jong-un. It is a country filled with rampant poverty, labor camps, human rights abuses, horrific atrocities, and crimes against its people. Now, this rogue nation is trying to flex its muscles by detonating hydrogen bombs and launching intercontinental ballistic missiles under the auspice of putting satellites in orbit.

It is a situation that does not allow for military action from the outset, as North Korea is a very irrational and unstable country. They are poised to launch a disproportionately large retaliatory strike for any transgression, be it real or imagined. North Korea maintains a "military first" policy that emphasizes all actions of the country are to boost its military. From agricultural production to technological advancements, the military is the primary beneficiary. It is a militaristic society that has no problem using military force. North Korea boasts the fourth largest standing military in the world, despite it being a country of only twenty-five million people.

The military is not North Korea's only weapon. They engage in cyber-warfare against its enemies and the United States. Remember the 2014 Sony hack over the movie *The Interview*? That was North Korea. North Korea became upset over a fictitious comedy that involved Seth Rogen and James Franco trying to assassinate Kim Jong-un. Their anger is understandable, but not cause to hack and damage a major movie studio.

Richard Haas, the president of the Council on Foreign Relations, wrote in the *Wall Street Journal* that we must enlist China in the fight to end the threat of North Korea.[68] China has become increasingly dissatisfied with the leadership of North Korea and views it as increasingly irrational. This view of growing instability and decreasing reliability as an ally has opened China up to being more open to neutralizing the threat that the North Korean regime presents. Haas continued in his piece:

> The priority must be to persuade China that the demise of North Korea need not be something to fear. Washington and Beijing should convene talks about how they could manage scenarios, including North Korean collapse and aggression. Nuclear weapons and materials would need to be secured. Governments need to make plans to ensure US, South Korean, and Chinese forces do not come into conflict.

At the same time, the "stick" of military force would have to be threatened in order to achieve our goal of a secure and stable North Korea. The use of force cannot be an idle threat. If it ever reached a point that American statements that we would use military options were not treated seriously, it would make it so that our own standing and ability to negotiate would be severely diminished. If that were to happen, few to no countries would engage in serious dialogue when it comes to issues of war and peace, as they know we would always opt for the latter. The former would carry no weight if it were ever mentioned.

What should be embraced is a foreign and national security policy that is based on the reality that we live in a dangerous world, but seek to make it a better place for all through diplomatic cooperation. Putting it another way, this foreign policy is best described with the saying, "I carry an umbrella because it could rain."

Millennials are proving to be contrarian when it comes to a key component in the War on Terror: they oppose drone strikes to eliminate terrorist targets. They are the only generation where the majority of them do not approve of drone strikes.[69] Minorities are also less likely to support drone strikes. They are close to securing a majority when it comes to disapproval.

Some have called drone strikes the future of warfare. If that is the future, millennials are not buying it. Oftentimes, when the American public hears about a drone strike on the news, it is because there were civilian casualties involving women and children. It is incredibly sad, but it is part of the risk we must take when launching such a strike. Remember, terrorists that are targeted for removal from the battlefield through a precision drone strike are quite intent on meeting their maker (and on taking as many innocents with them in the process). The men and women of the United States military are more than happy to provide members of ISIS and Al Qaeda with an introduction.

We cannot always let public opinion sway what we do when it comes to matters of national security. However, we can acknowledge the public's or a particular sector of the population's concerns and see if there is a way to make our strategy better than its current form. With drone strikes, we should consider utilizing more spotters on the ground when feasible; they could provide updated information and intelligence on whether or not civilians are at risk during a particular window for a strike. We can also use special forces teams to engage in special operations to either capture or eliminate terrorist threats. This would cut down on the number of drone strikes used, which President Obama used four times more than his predecessor, President George W. Bush.[70] Drone strikes being reduced in favor of special forces operations would not mean that the strikes could not be used—they should be when all other options are off the table.

The real problem that we confront with millennials when it comes to foreign policy is that they are less willing to take military action in order to bolster our national interests. Instead, they are more tolerant of hostile activities undertaken by others. It is a return to the isolationist roots of the United States, but not a viewpoint that can coexist with the reality of the dangers we face today.

What will register with millennials is if Republicans push to modernize our military. Again, technology is something that we understand and relate to in this day and age, so using innovation to bring about a stronger and more effective American military is in all of our interests.

Innovation and creation of new military technologies helps to create jobs and spur the American economy. It can also lead to many new products and technologies that can be used by the American public. Think about what products have been made possible by the drive for new military and space technologies. There are the inventions of Velcro, recreational drones, the Internet, GPS, duct tape, the EpiPen, the microwave, and the computer.[71] Most of these are products that we use in our daily lives and that Americans view as staples. Think about what military innovation can invent that we will use in our daily lives ten years from now—or twenty. That is exciting.

At the same time, we must closely monitor military spending. Just because we are authorizing military spending to focus on innovation does not mean that we should write a blank check to military developers. It will be imperative that Republicans adhere to their fiscally responsible roots and not fall victim to the common trap of never saying no to unwise spending on the military so as to not be painted as anti-military. Most elected officials on the right are terrified of being labeled as such. It could mean a primary challenge from their right flank or a tough general election battle with a moderate Democrat if they are in a competitive election. They should embrace the idea of saying no to wasting taxpayer dollars when it comes to military expenditures. If the technology or spending plan is ineffective or produces a product that does not work, then their opposition to it is, in fact, a way of strengthening our armed forces.

The world is a dangerous place that is filled with complexities. We do not have the luxury of living in a live-and-let-live bubble, as that will not keep us safe from terrorists and rogue nations. What will ensure the safety and security of Americans throughout the world is careful diplomacy, working with other nations to build international coalitions to combat terrorism and other problems throughout the world, and to always be ready to talk through our problems. At the same time, reality requires that we not be afraid to go at it alone and to use appropriate military force in order to solve a problem when other options are off the table. Millennials will respect and appreciate that tact, as the consequences of not doing so are too catastrophic to contemplate.

Chapter 12
Love, actually

GROWING UP IN NEW YORK CITY IS A UNIQUE EXPERIENCE. From day one, I was exposed to a wide variety of people, views, and lifestyles. It didn't make me more or less tolerant and accepting, but it did provide me with an environment where I had no reason to believe that there was anything wrong with people that are different than me. And there isn't. My prejudices weren't based on skin color or sexual orientation, but on likes. Red Sox fans were the target of my hatred (it was a rather playful bit of "screw you"), especially since I went to boarding school in Maine for high school where I had to constantly hear how "Nomaaar" Garciaparra, the shortstop for the Boston Red Sox, was basically the second coming of Jesus Christ. (Fact check: he wasn't.) Excusing the poor life choices (when it comes to baseball team preference) of Red Sox fans, they really aren't that different from anybody else. They are just people who are misguidedly passionate about an inferior baseball team. (Full disclosure: the New York Yankees are my team of choice.) Their lifestyle choices were their own and in no way impacted mine.

So when I was in college and a local club hockey team came calling, I said sure, I am more than happy to join—we all played at the same rink, after all. Then it got a bit weird for a minute. The guy asking me to join his team then asked if I was sure. They were a team for gays and lesbians. I asked does that mean they play hockey any differently? He said no, and I reaffirmed my commitment to play for their team. What did I care that my teammates were gay? I cared more about their skills on the ice and whether or not they were good people off the ice. And like that, I was the Jackie Robinson of straight people in gay hockey.

As it turned out, my teammates were some of the most fun people that I have ever played hockey with. They could skate, shoot, pass, hit, and bullshit with the best of them. Because I am straight, I was hazed (mainly with name calling including, "straighty," "breeder," "skirt chaser," etc.), but I survived the taunts and grew closer to my teammates. So when one day in 2004 the issue of gay marriage came up in a political debate I was involved in, I took my first public stand. I staunchly supported it. Who was I to tell my friends that they couldn't marry one another and build a stable home with the person they loved?

No party has successfully endured by continuing to push the ideas and policies of yesterday. In American politics today, both the Republican and Democratic parties are guilty of clinging to the past at the expense of their own future.

In order to make their own party's ideas palatable to an ever-shrinking voting public, each party attempts to undermine and diminish the other's platform and agenda through attack after attack. This occurs at every level of politics, from presidential race to local assembly race. As a result of portraying one's candidate or party as essentially the lesser of two evils, we see increased voter apathy and decreased participation.

Charles C. W. Cooke pointed out that:

> . . . conservatives have all too often tended to rely upon reflexive justifications that they might never accept in other areas, opening themselves up to charges of hypocrisy and

> weakening their cases with both their natural allies and with the independent voters that have customarily been the key to their success.

Cooke continues and rightly calls such thinking a "dangerous mistake."[72] He could not be more correct. Republicans, like Democrats, have adhered to their rigid positions without any belief that they must shift with the times. This has only turned off the electorate and permitted the party to drift further and further to the right.

Take for example the issue of marriage equality. In 2004, it was used as a wedge issue to help Republican candidates win in tight races. States across the country had placed ballot initiatives to ban same-sex marriage on their election slate. These ballot initiatives and the issue of terrorism pushed Republicans and swing voters into the GOP column and delivered major victories for the party. These wins were good for the party at the time, but seem to have cemented within members of the party the idea that opposing marriage equality is a road map to victory. Were this a decade ago, this would be a winning strategy to employ (though not one that would be morally right).

In 2005, a Gallup poll found that only 37 percent of Americans believed that gays and lesbians should be allowed to marry and 59 percent were against it. Within ten years, public opinion would literally flip with 60 percent of Americans being in favor of marriage equality and 37 percent opposed. Think about how drastic a shift that is within the public conscience. Few social issues have seen such a rapid and radical change in public opinion.

In 2015, millennial Republicans overwhelmingly supported marriage equality. To them, the ability of gays to marry was akin to African Americans being treated and protected equally under the law. Why wouldn't and shouldn't they be? Simply put, millennials view marriage equality as a civil rights issue. To them, it is in no way a wedge issue.

Look at how the issue of marriage equality has shifted over that ten-year period. The chart below from Gallup shows just how much the American people's view of gay marriage has changed in the past ten years.

Furthermore, 61 percent of millennial Republicans support marriage equality. Many of them have indicated that they would not vote for a candidate that does not support marriage equality. It does not matter to them if they sync up with the candidate on all other issues; if the candidate does not back marriage equality, the candidate will not receive the millennial vote, be it in a primary or general election.

Do you think marriages between same-sex couples should or should not be recognized by the law as valid, with the same rights as traditional marriages?

Trend in which gay marriage question preceded by questions on legality of gay/lesbian rights and relations

	Should be valid	Should not be valid	No opinion
	%	%	%
2015 May 6-10	60	37	3
2014 May 8-11	55	42	3
2013 Jul 10-14	54	43	3
2013 May 2-7	53	45	3
2012 Nov 26-29	53	46	2
2012 May 3-6	50	48	2
2011 Dec 15-18	48	48	4
2011 May 5-8	53	45	3
2010 May 3-6	44	53	3
2009 May 7-10	40	57	3
2008 May 8-11 †	40	56	4
2007 May 10-13	46	53	1
2006 May 8-11 †	42	56	2
2006 May 8-11 ^†	39	58	4
2005 Aug 22-25 ^	37	59	4
2004 May 2-4 ^	42	55	3
1999 Feb 8-9 ^	35	62	3
1996 Mar 15-17 ^	27	68	5

^WORDING: Do you think marriages between homosexuals should or should not be recognized by the law as valid, with the same rights as traditional marriages?
†Asked of a half sample

GALLUP'

Most Young Republicans Favor Same-Sex Marriage

Percent who favor allowing gays and lesbians to marry legally

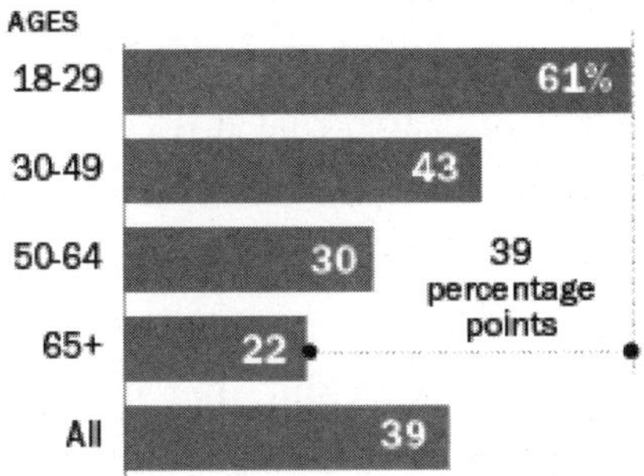

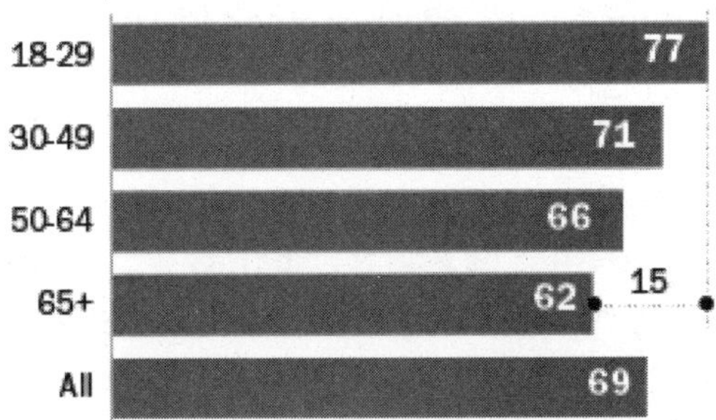

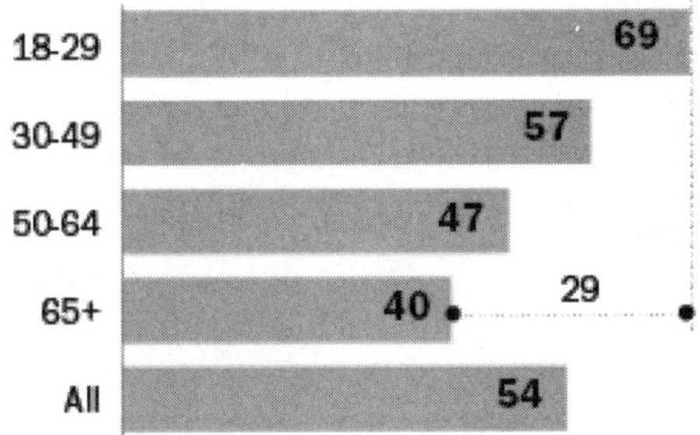

PEW RESEARCH CENTER

Millennial Democrats also overwhelmingly support marriage equality. A full 77 percent of them back it and, overall, 69 percent of millennials are in favor of gay marriage.

When it comes to the issue of gay families, millennial Republicans are on the exact same page as their Democratic counterparts. When asked whether a gay couple raising a child is a good thing, bad thing, or that it doesn't make a difference, 42 percent of millennial Republicans indicated that it doesn't make a difference. This is the same number as millennial Democrats. Essentially, 42 percent of millennials have said ¯_(ツ)_/¯ (the emoticon indicating a shrug of the shoulders) to gays and lesbians raising a child. Were they not allowed to raise a child, then it would be an issue. To us millennials, gays and lesbians raising children is a non-issue.

Gay and lesbian parents raising a child is a pro-family thing. They are providing kids with a stable and safe home in which to learn and become an adult. No, being gay is not a lifestyle choice or something

Few Young Republicans See Gay Families as Bad for Society

% who say more gay and lesbian couples raising children is a...

	Good thing	Bad thing	Doesn't make much difference/DK
	%	%	%
Total	25	33	43=100
Rep/Lean Rep	12	46	42=100
18-29	26	18	56=100
30-49	15	47	39=100
50-64	7	52	41=100
65+	3	66	32=100
Dem/Lean Dem	36	22	42=100
18-29	45	14	42=100
30-49	35	23	41=100
50-64	39	22	39=100
65+	17	32	51=100

Survey conducted Feb. 14-23, 2014. Figures may not add to 100% because of rounding.

PEW RESEARCH CENTER

that is acquired through proximity to somebody who happens to be homosexual. Statements such as that are ignorant and flat out wrong. Same-sex parents are more than capable of raising a child and instilling them with good and honest values. Society knows this to be true.

The social conservative wing of the Republican Party has allowed Democrats to paint Republicans as some sort of self-righteous and patronizing religious group that seeks to instill their values on the rest of the country. To them, religious and social conservatives might as well be some sort of a cult that is the very definition of intolerance, especially toward gays. They are some form of a political boogeyman.

At the same time that millennials and the country have become more accepting of gays and equal rights, so too have Christians in the United States. Part of this acceptance is due to the fact that gays and lesbians are found throughout our ranks. They are our brothers, sisters, cousins, aunts, uncles, sons, and daughters. We, as a nation, have become increasingly more accepting of people that are different from us.

In August of 2015, Republican presidential candidate John Kasich, the governor of Ohio, was asked about his views on gay marriage in the first Republican presidential debate. He has long and publicly held that he believes that marriage should be between a man and a woman.

> Well, look, I'm an old-fashioned person here, and I happen to believe in traditional marriage. But I've also said the court has ruled . . . and I said we'll accept it. And guess what, I just went to the wedding of a friend of mine who happens to be gay. Because somebody doesn't think the way I do doesn't mean that I can't care about them or I can't love them. So, if one of my daughters happened to be that, of course I would love them, and I would accept them, because you know what, that's what we're taught when we have strong faith. Issues like that are planted to divide us. . . . We need to give everybody a chance, treat everybody with respect, and let them share in this great American dream that we have.

> Megyn, I'm going to love my daughters; I'm going to love them no matter what they do, because you know what? God gives me unconditional love. I'm going to give it to my family and my friends and the people around me.[73]

The answer reflects a level of pragmatism and the embrace of reality that Republicans should adopt. Not only was it widely praised from most corners of the country, it demonstrated that the Republican Party is not composed of the intolerant monsters that the left often portrays us to be.

Has the Republican Party overall adapted to this shift in the electorate? Not really. Today, we still have mainstream candidates calling the Supreme Court's decision allowing same-sex marriage a travesty, and some go so far as to call for a constitutional amendment that defines marriage as a union between one man and one woman. They often cite gay marriage as a slippery slope to allowing a man to marry a sheep—begging the question of how the sheep would consent to such a union—or even a father marrying his own daughter. Both are ridiculous ways of hiding the fact that they really just are not comfortable with our gay and lesbian brothers and sisters marrying. This belief does not adapt to the changing circumstances and opinion of the American people. Nor does it recognize the beliefs on the matter of the overwhelming majority of Republican millennials.

In 2016, marriage equality is not an issue on the campaign trail. Both Democrats and Republicans have largely glossed over it, and that is assuming they address it at all. Just because the Supreme Court ruled on it does not mean it is a dead issue. People still care about the issue and view it as a basic civil right. A comparable era would be after right after the passage of the Civil Rights Act in 1964. It outlawed discrimination based on race, color, religion, sex, or national origin. African Americans and other minorities finally received the long overdue legal equality to which they were entitled. In the election of 1964, mainstream candidates didn't hit the

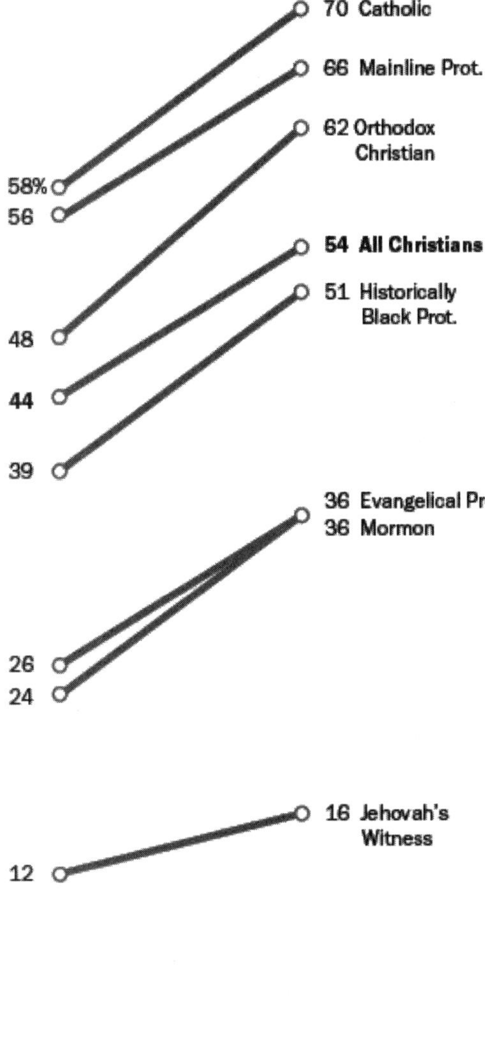
Almost all Christian groups now more accepting of homosexuality
% saying homosexuality should be accepted by society
70 Catholic
66 Mainline Prot.
62 Orthodox Christian
54 All Christians
51 Historically Black Prot.
36 Evangelical Prot.
36 Mormon
16 Jehovah's Witness
58%
56
48
44
39
26
24
12
2007
2014
Source: 2014 Religious Landscape Study, conducted June 4-Sept. 30, 2014.
PEW RESEARCH CENTER

campaign trail and promise to repeal the Civil Rights Act or propose policies that would legally classify a certain segment of the population as second-class citizens. In this sense, the election of 2016 is the same as the election of 1964.

There is a simple fix here. The Republican Party simply adapts and evolves to the changing times and opinions of Americans and the electorate. How does it do this? First, we must start by having the party adopt a gay-friendly platform that begins to show that we are not an anti-gay party. The news of such a move by the party would get the ball rolling on all facets of the party shifting. It would be, in essence, a trickle-down change in party thinking. Next, party members, institutions, and structures should focus on promoting candidates who support marriage equality, or at least not oppose it.

Going further, we should adopt the tone and pragmatic view of John Kasich. It has the power to resonate with the electorate and stun those who believe us to be rigid religious zealots. Imagine the power of Republicans across the country all taking the Kasich position. Americans, especially millennials, would certainly take note of this shift.

Of course, how we frame the seemingly sudden switch will be important. If we solely state that this is the right thing to do or that we recognize the shifting electorate, then there will be charges that we Republicans have abandoned our "moral high ground" or our values are flexible (again, part of the national caricature created by the left and the subjective media). However, if we make this change in attitude toward marriage equality in an economically conservative manner, particularly one that adheres to the principles of the free market and highlights how gay marriage is an economic win for all, then we have a legitimate narrative for how the GOP "evolved" on the issue.

So how in the hell is marriage equality an economic win? First of all, have you ever seen the bill for a wedding? Even a small one is at minimum a five-figure expenditure with venue rental, catering, florists, photographers, dress, DJ, etc. It might be a reason your trustworthy author secretly hopes that he has only sons, as the bride's father is on the hook for at least the equivalent of a couple of years of college tuition . . . that is spent in one night. It may sound silly, but weddings are a legitimate economic stimulus package for local economies. They create jobs by employing the DJ, the caterer, the florist, and others.

Republicans should also emphasize that marriage equality is a civil rights issue. If two men or two women wish to marry one another, it in no way harms them or the people around them. We should adhere to the guidelines of Dr. Martin Luther King Jr. who advised us all to judge people not based on the color of their skin, but the content of their character. Were Dr. King alive today, it's a good bet that he would expand this to include sexual orientation. At the end of the day, it all boils down to the question, "Is this person a good person?" Whether or not that person is heterosexual or homosexual should not impact the answer to that question.

At the same time, we must be flexible and recognize that some members of the party will not willingly shift their position on the issue of marriage equality. They should be allowed to have their views, as the United States of America is a country founded on the protection of the minority opinion. However, we must quietly discourage the members of the party who hold this minority outlook on marriage equality from being vocal about it. Respecting their right to disagree is important to our showing tolerance to differing beliefs.

Chapter 13
What is the safe word in my safe space?

WHEN I WAS COMPLETING MY UNDERGRADUATE DEGREE AT Fordham University, the second Iraq War was just about to begin. Students who were politically active overwhelmingly protested the (at the time) potential war, arguing that it was a way for President Bush and Vice President Cheney to make a good deal of money for their corporate backers and friends. "No blood for oil!" they would chant at rallies outside the cafeteria. I would be accosted by them, as they, like most kids in a liberal arts university, underwent their political awakening. There was not a strong Republican presence at Fordham, but the College Democrats at Fordham University were there and ready to organize.

The looming Iraq War was all that anybody could talk about on campus. Whether it was in class or at the local watering hole on dollar beer night, there was the familiar refrain: "We have to do something to stop this war from starting." One classmate exclaimed to me that even though the war was a sure thing, she was going to protest so that "history would remember that the world was against mindless greed and slaughter." At the time, I was far less conservative than I am today and had a bit of a liberal rebellious streak in me. Despite this, I supported the Iraq War, but not for the reasons President Bush had pitched the American people. The two most influential parts of my foreign policy beliefs, 9/11 and the Holocaust, screamed at me that removing Saddam Hussein from power was not only the right thing to do, it was the moral thing to do.

Late one Wednesday morning in the fall of 2002, I was headed to class when a classmate approached me. He stridently walked up to me and said, "Don't you want to stop the war?!" I wasn't sure how to react. Perhaps it was because I was still half asleep and not in any state to engage in any serious thought, but I didn't understand the question. I could only register a shocked and blank look.

He queried me again, "Shouldn't we drop books and not bombs?!" That sure as hell woke me up.

"You mean that we should literally drop books on the Iraqi people?" I asked.

"Damn right, we should," my new protesting friend exclaimed. I began to laugh, primarily because I realized this guy was an idiot. His clothes reeked of weed and of a few weeks of not being laundered.

"You realize that if we literally dropped books on people from several thousand feet, the books would achieve a velocity that would sufficiently cause the person hit to turn to goo, right?" I said. With that, my solicitor stammered a few unintelligible words and grunts, and walked back to the table he was manning that had all of the demonstration material.

To this day, I can't help but laugh at this encounter. This guy, who was perfectly well meaning, could barely understand the implications of what he was saying. Here was a situation where a brutal dictator was oppressing his own people, and the solution of this classmate was to drop physical books on the Iraqi people. Forget the danger these books posed as falling objects; the truly ludicrous aspect of his approach was that education would solve the problem of Saddam Hussein. For me, it reinforced my belief that while the antiwar movement means well, they take an overly simplistic view of the very complex world in which we live.

There is the old adage that the reason kids in college protest is because they want to get laid. This is based on some truth. If you show you are passionate enough about something, you might be playing a game of naked Twister with somebody you fancy! College certainly is liberating, no? Each and every time I have set foot on a college campus since I graduated, the situation has remained the same. Students are experiencing their political awakening and want to make a difference. For some, it's because they want to make a difference; idealism has yet to leave them. Others just want to get lucky. No matter the motivation, there is a hunger to achieve and we damn well should feed it.

The year 2015 was a banner year for college students. They all seemed to switch their majors to demonstrating against whatever mundane thing they felt threatened their personal feelings. A decade ago, people would protest to get laid; now they protest to avoid being protested for not protesting. The people demonstrating? Younger millennials.

College protests in 2015 can be traced back to September 2011, when a group known as Occupy Wall Street (who were a result of the Great Recession) began to protest what it believed to be threats to the United States: income inequality, greed, corporate influence, and social inequality. They repeatedly stated that, "We are the ninety-nine percent" and they were representing all Americans in the fight against the 1 percent that they believed controlled everything. Occupy Wall Street employed tactics of social disruption by camping out 24/7 in downtown New York's Zuccotti Park. The location was smack dab in the heart of the New York City financial community and blocks away from New York City Hall. They were a visible presence that could not be ignored, no matter how hard one tried.

The demographics of Occupy Wall Street were overwhelmingly millennials. Sixty-four percent of the people involved were under

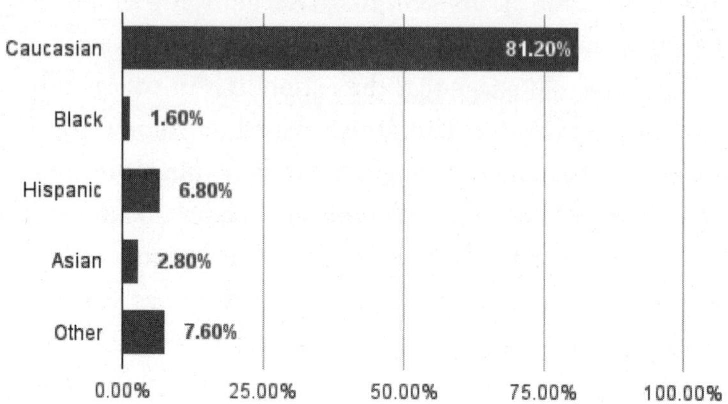

the age of thirty-four. When it came to race, whites were by far the most active ethnicity involved in the movement. They claimed to be a microcosm of the 99 percent of people in the United States, but they were anything but.

When it came to party leanings, the results were somewhat surprising. The vast majority of Occupy Wall Street members considered themselves to be independent, not Republican or Democrat.[74] Occupy Wall Street indirectly evolved into the Black Lives Matter movement, which was a reaction to the deaths of African American men at the hands of law enforcement, as well as the perceived social injustice faced by blacks today. At present, no substantive details exist about the demographics of the Black Lives Matter movement, but looking at its history and publicly available information, one can deduce that the racial disparity seen in the Occupy Wall Street movement is not at play here. African Americans seem to be the majority with whites as the second largest ethnic group.

The Black Lives Matter movement grew when grand juries chose not to indict the police officers involved in the deaths of Ferguson, Missouri resident Michael Brown and Staten Islander Eric Garner.

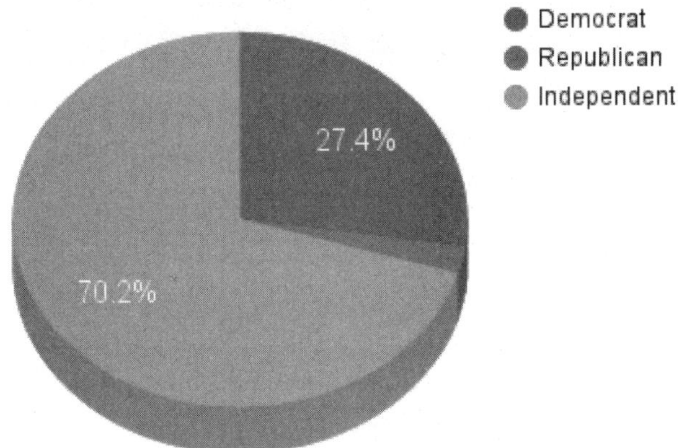

Both grand juries declined to indict within eight days of one another. This set off a year of tensions and the powder keg exploded.

Marchers brazenly attempted to shut down streets and public areas by literally inserting themselves into them. They were human obstructions and they would not be deterred. Soon, protesters began to call not just for change to the criminal justice system, but for violence against police officers. Next, members of the NYPD were assaulted by demonstrators on the Brooklyn Bridge. It was a matter of time before things would get even more out of control.

On a cold afternoon on the Saturday before Christmas, two of New York's Finest were sitting in their patrol car, protecting the people of Bedford-Stuyvesant, Brooklyn. Police officers Wenjian Liu and Rafael Ramos were far removed from the protests and the action that had occupied the city for three weeks. Liu, a Chinese immigrant and seven-year veteran of the NYPD, had gotten married just two months before. Ramos, a spiritual man, was married with two sons. He was training to become a volunteer chaplain and planned to join the ministry after he retired from the NYPD. It was December 20, 2014.

To Ismaaiyl Abdullah Brinsley, Rafael Ramos and Wenjian Liu were part of the problem confronting America. They couldn't just be punched by protesters; they had to be given a more severe punishment. To Brinsley, they also were responsible for the deaths of Michael Brown and Eric Garner. They represented the system that targeted black men. They had to pay. Brinsley walked up to their patrol car, aimed his Taurus PT92 handgun, and pulled the trigger. The time was 2:47 p.m.

The assassination of Liu and Ramos caused many to recoil in horror. The protests paused out of respect. Christmas and New Year's came, as did brutal cold. Many began asking why we let things go so far. The answer was simple: elected leaders within these urban areas, all Democrats, had turned a blind eye toward the protests as they escalated in severity. Leaders, such as New York City Mayor Bill de Blasio, did not want to offend their core constituencies who had veered further and further left after Republicans had chosen to no longer pursue their support and vote.

Another area that went off the rails due to Democratic control with no effective Republican counterbalance was Baltimore. Following the death of Freddie Gray while in the custody of the Baltimore Police Department, the city imploded. Years of neglect, failed urban policy, high crime, and one party rule had perfectly primed Baltimore to be the next urban area that erupted in outrage. Baltimore was Ferguson on steroids. Stores burned. The city was paralyzed. Disobedience and chaos reigned.

In his piece in the Manhattan Institute's *City Journal*, "The Riot Ideology, Reborn," Fred Siegel notes:

> In the wake of the 2014 riots in Ferguson, Missouri, and the 2015 West Baltimore riots, a new riot ideology has taken hold, one similarly intoxicated with violence and willing to excuse it but with a different goal.[75]

Rioters were not pushing a social justice agenda; rather they were reveling in the anarchy that they had caused. At the same time, there were protesters who felt strongly that significant problems were within the current governing structure that needed to be addressed.

This is not to legitimize their grievances, nor delegitimize them. However, the people who most wanted change were more than happy to step aside and allow the violence and rioting to run rampant.

The nonviolent elements of these social justice movement groups found that it served their goal of getting attention from the media to permit and enable the out-of-control rioters to destroy Baltimore. The more Baltimore burned, the more frantically the press wanted to talk to them. They were able to stand on their soapbox and preach their views on the state of things while the media greedily consumed each and every word. A lesson was to be learned here by those who wanted to push a movement in the future: traditional protests no longer achieved the attention desired.

The only way to get media attention was through extreme action. College students took this lesson to heart and in the fall of 2015, they began their own social crusades across the country.

Many college students, and people just about to enter college, were becoming socially aware during the period of winter, spring, and summer of 2015. As they came to their college campuses in August and September 2015, there was a feeling that they needed to do something, anything for that matter, that continued to demonstrate their social awareness and genuine desire to make a positive impact.

For most, going away to college is the first time that most young people have lived away from home and have been independent. It can be a rather liberating experience, but it can also be overwhelming, especially since this generation, the younger millennials, have had parents who sought to protect and shield them from the harsh realities of the real world. Their systems were shocked and they responded in the only way they knew how: to demand that they feel insulated and safe from the bad.

Any and everything was the cause of alarm. Students at the University of Missouri began their protests on September 24, 2015. Payton Head, the president of the student government, stated that a culture of bigotry and anti-gay sentiment existed on campus.

The protesters alleged that the university's administration didn't take racism seriously and that their actions only perpetuated it. They then went further and protested the loss of health insurance for graduate students.

In August of 2015, the university informed graduate students that

> Due to changes in federal policy and IRS interpretation of that policy, general counsel has informed us that the University of Missouri no longer is allowed to pay for graduate students' health insurance. (Previously, the university provided a subsidy to those students who opted in for insurance and were paid from a qualifying assistantship or fellowship.) The IRS considers our student health insurance plan an "individual-market plan" rather than an "employer-sponsored plan," such as our health plans for MU employees.
>
> The Affordable Care Act prevents employers from giving employees money specifically so they can buy health insurance on the individual market. Graduate teaching and research assistants are classified as employees by the IRS, so they fall under this ruling.[76]

Why did they cancel health insurance for graduate students? Obamacare. We conservatives warned that while Obamacare was well-intentioned, its consequences would be vast and would negatively impact many Americans. Protesters blamed the University of Missouri. They did not assign any responsibility to President Obama or the Democrats who championed Obamacare and made it so that the university legally could not provide health coverage for graduate students. The logic of protesting the University of Missouri and its administration was baffling.

What the loss of health insurance did do for the student demonstrators was enable them to add a legitimate issue to their illegitimate list of demands. Their original demands were that the

University of Missouri take instances of racism more seriously than they already did and that they provide a more culturally sensitive, if not more insulated, environment than the one that existed at the time. It was not a big draw for the press to just deal with the hurt feelings of young millennials, but once they added a major issue to the fold, whoa Nelly . . . the fight transformed into one that took on legitimate and important dimensions—ones that had been the direct result of combative political debate that had revealed a schism within the country. The Obamacare debate had entered a new phase.

This time, like they did in prior instances, Republicans made a mistake in how to approach the protestors. The GOP's error was in that they did not even bother to reach out to the demonstrators. Instead, we ignored and dismissed their concerns. Making matters worse, many Republicans used the opportunity to chest-thump by publicly insulting these groups.

Many Republicans made counterproductive and incendiary remarks about Black Lives Matter and other movements. Wisconsin Governor Scott Walker compared protesters to ISIS when he boasted that taking them on prepared him to be Commander in Chief. After a Black Lives Matter member was ejected from a Donald Trump presidential rally in November 2015, Trump said in an interview:

> Maybe he should have been roughed up, because it was absolutely disgusting what he was doing,[77]

In early 2016, Trump supporters began to get violent with people who protested at his campaign rallies. In March 2016, a man was being led out of a Trump rally after he had demonstrated against Trump. Video captured the moment a Trump backer walked up to him and sucker punched him in the face. He was later interviewed and told the press that the protester deserved it and that next time he should be killed. The response of Donald Trump? He did not disavow the violent actions of his supporter or appeal for calm at his rallies.

Trump said that his fans were really patriotic and it was understandable that they had chosen to show their feelings of frustration with the system. Essentially, Trump ridiculously argued that his supporters loved their country so much that their patriotism would manifest itself in the form of physical violence. America, f&%k yeah!

Thankfully, some younger Republican elected officials were wiser in their choice of words. South Carolina Governor Nikki Haley discussed the devastation in Baltimore in a more practical and relatable manner:

> Most of the people killed or injured in the riots in Ferguson and Baltimore were black. Most of the small businesses or social service institutions that were destroyed and looted in Ferguson and Baltimore were either black-owned or served heavily black populations. Most of the people who now live in terror because local police are too intimidated to do their jobs are black. Black lives do matter, and they have been disgracefully jeopardized by the movement that has laid waste to Ferguson and Baltimore.[78]

As a result of their demands to be given significant oversight of government entities and college campuses, it has been suggested that the Black Lives Matter and college campus protesters are basically the inmates begging to run the asylum. This is not exactly true. In reality, this is much more of a situation where the visitors are asking to run the asylum. Black Lives Matter members are not inmates, but rather are concerned with the people running the institution. The shootings that they protest, more likely than not, occurred in poorer neighborhoods that are primarily minority. Not exactly the most receptive area for a GOP message, but that's to be expected because of the Republican Party's ceding of these areas years ago. Democratic dominance and policies have damaged these areas with poor education, high taxes, and many other negative conditions.

The college protesters are not inmates in an asylum either. A more fitting analogy would be that they are members of an elite health club. They spend a copious amount of money—each student ends up owing an average of $31,000 at the time of graduation—annually in exchange for access to a service (education). They have every right to complain about the conditions on campus, but they do not have the right to do so in a manner that detracts from the experience of others. Furthermore, these student protesters must recognize that they possess the ability to extricate themselves from the situation that they so strenuously object to. Yes, they are fully able to opt out and cease supporting the educational institution through their tuition.

So what does this all have to do with Republicans and conservatives? This is an opportunity to truly reach out and recruit millennials to our ranks. We can uniquely show courage and attempt to convert these students and millennials to our ideas and solutions. But, if Republicans are to do this, they must first prove themselves worthy of being listened to by the protesters. They must sit down with these activists and not only hear what they have to say, but understand what they are saying. This doesn't mean that members of the GOP have to agree, but we must respect the opinions of members of movements such as Black Lives Matter. This will achieve remarkable results and foster a mutual respect between activists and Republicans.

There is no doubt that such an undertaking will take time, effort, and money, all resources that the old guard of the GOP is reluctant to part with for this cause. They remain stuck in the mindset that we should win for today at the expense of building for tomorrow.

First off, we should begin a dialogue with the people who feel that they have been wronged and who are victims of a system that has not benefited them since at least the 1990s. Conveniently for us Republicans, this system has largely been controlled and implemented by Democrats. At the same time, this does not make the argument that Republicans should be listened to and trusted any easier with these target groups. They are not likely to immediately embrace a group of people that have been caricatured by the left and media as the boogeyman of American politics. Some will never accept or trust us, as, to them, the GOP is the enemy and does not care about them. Yet, we must press on and seek to change the perception. It is better to have tried and failed than having failed to try.

The place to start changing the minds of Black Lives Matter activists and others is with the issue of body cameras on police officers. This is a policy that has every police officer wearing a camera on his or her uniform that records all interactions with suspects. Already, body cameras are showing their benefits, with police officers having been charged with crimes. In November 2015, two African American police officers in Louisiana were charged with murder for the killing of Jeremy Mardis, a white six-year-old boy.[79] The reason for the murder charges? The body camera footage of one of the officers showed that the officers fired eighteen shots at the boy and his father. Both were unarmed. In January 2016, body cameras again proved their worth when the United States Department of Justice filed civil rights violation charges against a Las Vegas police officer who used excessive force against a woman and then tried to cover it up.[80] The evidence of this? Again, footage that was shot by the officer's own body camera.

To many civil libertarians, police body cameras are an invasion of privacy and a shining example of "Big Government" run amok. Some even call it a form of illegal search and seizure. After all, it is the government taking a set of data or facts in the form of a video of a person's activity. Shouldn't a judge be required to sign off on the recording of this footage? No.

Let's go over what type of footage body cameras would actually record. They would document the routine interactions between the officer and potential suspect. These engagements would occur either in public space, where it is perfectly legal for citizens to film police officers or whatever they like, or in a private space where the officer is entering either due to a warrant or due to probable cause. If anything, the footage for entering a private area under the pretense of probable cause allows the police to further prove their case that the situation warranted intervention. The same is true for defendants and their defense counsel who might allege wrongdoing and seek to have charges dismissed based on the officer not following proper procedure.

Police body cameras only build trust between the public and the police, especially in a time when it is sorely needed. They would serve as a layer of insurance and an unbiased record of what happened during a police encounter where one side is alleging misconduct against the other. Millennials and urban minorities have been asking that the police use this technology to improve the policing experience. Why not give them what they want in cities like New York, Boston, Los Angeles, and Chicago?

Then there is the benefit of how body camera footage will positively impact police officers. To hear Black Lives Matter protesters and others tell it, police forces across the United States are perpetrating some sort of organized undertaking against minorities. They are engaged in a full-scale campaign of terror for some unexplained reason. It's false and drives many Independents and Republicans, including myself, away from the conversation about sensible police reform. Portraying police departments and their upstanding officers in such a negative light only harms the cause that they claim to champion and makes people not engage in the discussion of police reform, but to rebut the outrageous charges against the police.

Instead of battling over this, embracing police body cameras enable pro-police advocates to hit back and use objective facts to refute claims of massive and system-wide police violence. Each and every police encounter that is facing a complaint from the public can be reviewed by the pre-existing police complaint organizations, such as New York City's Civilian Complaint Review Board. Irrefutable video evidence will facilitate a decrease in complaints against the police. With that, the false narrative that cops are targeting minorities can begin to go away and restore police officers to the position of esteem that they once held.

You don't believe that it is possible that police body cameras have utility in that they can clarify what exactly happened? Let's look at Melissa Click, a professor at the University of Missouri. In February 2016, video emerged of Professor Click yelling and cursing at police officers at the University of Missouri's homecoming parade in October 2015. This unbiased footage caused the university to convene a hearing to see if disciplinary action against her was warranted.[81]

If anything, millennials would view police departments' embrace of new technology in order to better serve the people who they protect as cool. Remember, millennials are incredibly technology-oriented. They also are more socially conscious and believe that every citizen deserves equal treatment under the law.

Another emerging issue is sentencing reform. Much has been made about the fact that the current federal sentencing guidelines disproportionately penalize minorities, especially when it comes to drug convictions. The sentences passed down to people found in possession of crack cocaine are harsher than those given to people who are convicted of possessing powdered cocaine. The poor and minorities are more likely to use crack cocaine than they are powdered due to it being less expensive and more readily available. Powdered cocaine, on the other hand, is far more expensive and a drug that affluent whites will use. It's essentially a rich man's drug. Let's do something about this disparity.

Republicans can propose commonsense revisions to the federal sentencing guidelines that make it so there is more fairness and equality for all who commit crimes. Many federal judges have spoken out about how their hands are tied in how they can sentence a convicted defendant when the law dictates the minimum sentencing. These mandatory minimum sentencing guidelines inhibit and prevent judges from taking extenuating circumstances into consideration. The solution is for Republicans to push reform that allows judges to sentence either more or less time in prison to convicted felons based upon the circumstances of the crime they committed. Other reforms that Republicans could champion are known as "legislative safety valves." These allow judges to give defendants sentences that are less than the mandatory minimum. However, the defendant would have to meet a certain set of predetermined criteria.

Now that Republicans have demonstrated a commitment to social justice through police modernization and sentencing reforms, our street credibility (for lack of a better term) will allow us to discuss other important matters with millennials and urban residents. Where is it better to start than on the issue of education?

Three days before the 2016 South Carolina Republican primary, CNN hosted a town hall event with many of the GOP presidential candidates. Each candidate was interviewed by Anderson Cooper, who asked some rather difficult and uncomfortable questions. Marco Rubio, who had just had a disappointing finish in the New Hampshire primary, received a rather uncomfortable question for any Republican: a question about race relations in the United States. Rubio then said:

> But I also know—but I also know that there are communities in this country where minority communities and the police department have a terrible relationship. I personally know someone who happens to be a police officer and a young African American male, who told me that he has been pulled over seven, eight times in the last four years and never gets a ticket.
>
> What is he supposed to think?
>
> He gets pulled over for no reason, never gets a ticket; no one has any explanation for why he's being pulled over.
>
> What is he supposed to think?
>
> So I also know that in this country, there is a significant number, particularly of young African American males, who feel as if they're treated differently than the rest of society.

And here's the bottom line, whether you agree with them or not, I happen to have seen this happen.

But whether you agree with them or not, if a significant percentage of the American family believes that they are being treated differently than everyone else, we have a problem. And we have to address it as a society and as a country, because I do not believe we can fulfill our potential as a nation unless we address that.

I'm not sure there's a political solution that they are being treated differently than everyone else. We have a problem and we have to address it as a society and as a country because I do not believe that we can fulfill our potential as a nation unless we address that.

I'm not sure it [*sic*] there's a political solution to that problem but there are things we can do. For example, one of the reasons why you see both educational and academic underperformance—not just in the African American community but also in the Hispanic community—is because of how a disproportionate number of our children are growing up in broken homes and dangerous neighborhoods.

They're living in substandard housing and forced by the government to attend a failing school. A child that's born with four strikes against them is going to struggle to succeed unless something breaks that cycle. We've seen things that work.

In New York City, Jeffrey Canada and the Harlem Children's Zone has shown us what works. You get involved in the lives of children and you begin to address those strikes against them. And you can see the same results you would get anywhere else in the country.

So I do believe as a society, we have to confront this issue in a responsible way because ultimately, if a significant percentage of the American feels that they are locked out of the promise of America, we will never be able to fulfill our destiny as a great nation.[82]

Marco Rubio provided perhaps the best answer on race relations in the United States that a Republican presidential candidate has ever given. It was a stunning response that connected with the audience and the viewer. Rubio effectively communicated that we must give our children safer neighborhoods and a higher quality of education. What is the thing that allows people to pull themselves up the ladder of opportunity? Education.

Chapter 14
Is it just me, or is it hot in here?

"Hey, buddy, can you spare a moment to help the environment?"

If you are like me, you will recognize this as a common refrain of the clipboard carrying members of Greenpeace and other environmental organizations. They stand out on the streets of New York, Boston, Chicago, Los Angeles, New Orleans, etc. and ask every person who passes by this simple question. They are the urban street version of telemarketers.

For me, there is only one way to deal with these people, as neither the polite decline nor simply walking past them without saying anything does not deter these solicitors. I respond with the line, "Thanks, but I am a Republican." It does the trick as they think that I am somehow anti-environment and they have no idea how to respond.

Today, the Republican Party is viewed as reacting to science by saying, "Yeah, the jury is still out on that science thing." That is not a good thing to be known for, especially when we live in a world where science is responsible for so much innovation and creation that resulted in products that we use in our daily lives. Electricity that powers our iPhones? Science. The medicine that is promoted by that bee voiced by Antonio Banderas on television (Nasonex)? Science. Nuclear power? Science.

Science has been at the core of American innovation and made man's dream of reaching the stars become a reality. The progress that humanity has made in the past one hundred years is remarkable and the United States of America has played a key role in the vast majority of these major advances.

It was Richard Nixon, a Republican president, who created the Environmental Protection Agency on December 2, 1970. Its goal was to streamline the broken and often confusing array of environmental laws enacted by states and local communities. The goal of the Environmental Protection Agency was (and still is) to protect human health and the environment. Noble goals.

Republicans have a history of being pro-science and stewards of the environment. It was President Theodore Roosevelt who created the National Parks Service when he signed the Antiquities Act in 1906. Now, over one hundred years later, the national parks are an institution and part of the fabric of the United States. It was also President Ronald Reagan, a hero of the Republican Party, who proposed that we combat acid rain by reducing emissions that contributed to the problem. Reagan considered himself an environmentalist and pushed for a commonsense approach when it came to the environment. This is the same approach that Republicans should take now. As Eli Lehrer wrote of President Reagan's environmental record in the *Weekly Standard*:

> A classic example of Reagan's approach can be found in the Coastal Barrier Resources Act, which the president signed in 1982. The law established the Coastal Barrier Resources System (CBRS), a zone that today encompasses 273 million acres of land (an area larger than all but one national park in the lower forty-eight states) in which federal subsidies to new development—notably, subsidies for roads, housing,

and flood insurance—are forbidden. Private interests may still develop the land but must do so without a penny of federal money. It is estimated the law has saved taxpayers $1 billion since its enactment.[83]

Ronald Reagan understood that being pro-environment is also fiscally conservative and responsible. As they say, the proof is in the pudding and Lehrer points out that Reagan's Coastal Barrier Resources Act was good for the taxpayer. And this was just the positive result of a single act that was good for the environment. Imagine how many taxpayer dollars could be saved if we used President Reagan's approach when it came to climate change?

Seventy-six percent of Americans believe that climate change is occurring. Only 14 percent deny that it is even happening. Yet, some within the Republican Party seek to cast doubt on established scientific fact. These voices of denial only get loud whenever we try to engage in a national discussion about climate change and what to do about it. They do so despite overwhelming evidence that debunks their particular viewpoint.

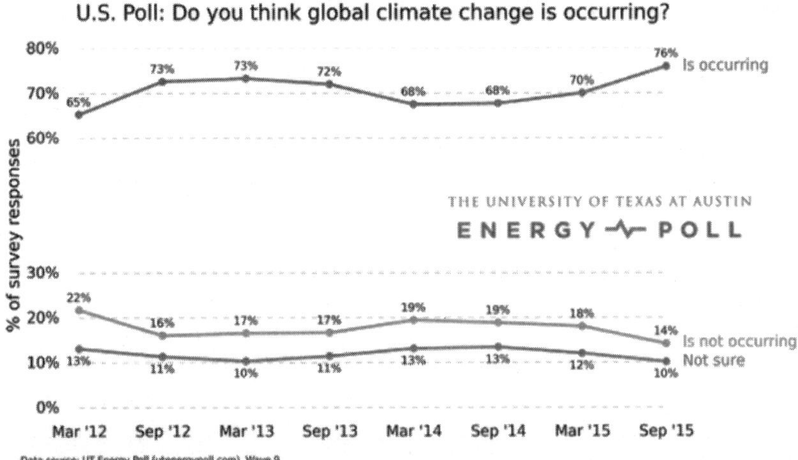

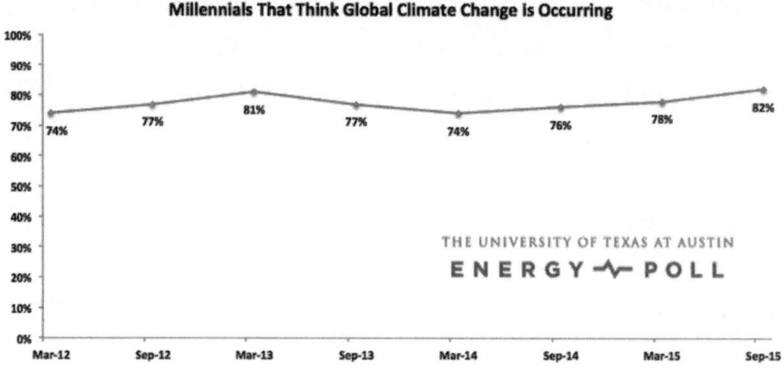

When it comes to millennials, 82 percent believe that climate change is happening. Among Republicans, that figure is 59 percent.

So why are Republicans allowing the party to disparage and cast doubt on climate change? What good does it do us as a party to debate whether or not it is really happening? Instead, we should be talking about solutions to the problem of climate change. In January 2015, the United States Senate voted ninety-eight to one to acknowledge that climate change is happening.[84] Even the most ardent climate change skeptics, including Republican Senator James Inhofe of Oklahoma, voted in favor of stating that climate change is happening. Where the senators differed was in the root cause of the problem.

As part of the transition from doubting climate change, Republicans should convert skeptics by pointing out the financial gains that the United States, its companies, and its citizens could make. Starting with local consumers, the GOP should highlight how they can not only switch the source of their energy to be better for the environment, but they can make money in doing it. Renewable energy offers such an opportunity for all.

Denmark has used alternative and renewable energy to empower its citizens to not only be able to produce their own energy, but sell excess energy back to power companies at above-market rate. The excess energy is stored on public power grids and then sold by the power companies to other consumers. This has contributed to

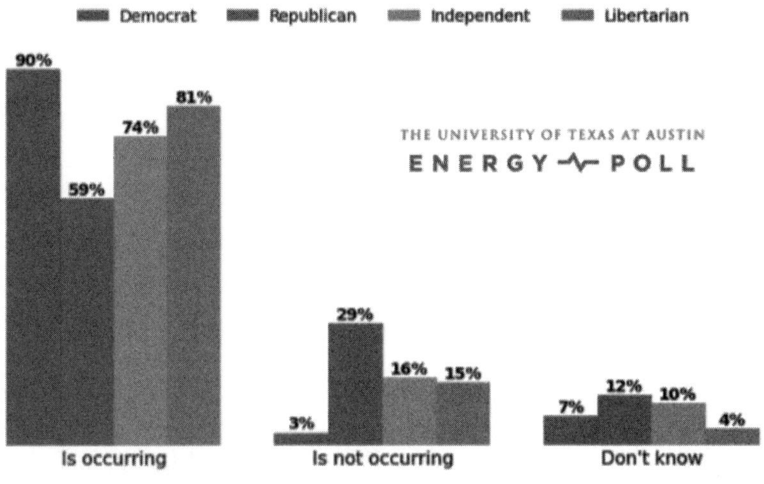

Denmark's power supply being 35 percent renewable energy by 2020 and 100 percent renewable energy by 2050. The Danish people were able to lessen their own energy costs by producing their own power and earn extra money in the process. How? Solar power. Danes installed solar panels on their homes and literally basked in the profits.

Solar power is just one of many methods of clean energy production that the United States can turn toward. It isn't particularly effective in a city such as New York City, where living spaces are small and having a four foot by six foot balcony is considered a luxury. Individual New Yorkers won't be able to follow the lead of the Danes and produce their own power by placing solar panels on the exterior of their apartments. Many apartment buildings do not offer sufficient access to the amount of sunlight required to fuel these panels. However, the roofs of the buildings, especially high-rises, can offer enough exposure to sunlight so that solar panels would be a somewhat viable option. Unfortunately, this would not provide sufficient energy to power the high-rise apartment buildings of New York, Chicago, and Boston.

As urban centers grow and develop, a new and trendy style of building is emerging: the all-glass tower. This offers an opportunity for developers to make use of a new and emerging technology, transparent solar panels that look and function exactly like glass.[85] This provides an opportunity for Republicans to encourage developers in urban areas to make use of this technology. We should use highly sought after real estate tax abatements as the incentive to adopt new technology that provides alternative energy.

There are other forms of alternative energy that can be encouraged by Republicans. In the plains states, wind power offers a significant benefit to its residents. Obviously, it is not a wise idea to establish wind turbines and farms in cities, but the areas just outside of them would prove ideal for wind power. These wind farms would provide clean energy and jobs for urban residents.

Democrats love to talk about ending our dependence on fossil fuels. They often argue that if we just had the will, then the country could immediately switch from pollutant-causing power sources to clean energy. That's not exactly true. The transition to clean and renewable energy will take a while as the technology is developed and implemented. The very energy sources that Democrats and environmentalists would like to get rid of will still be necessary for ensuring that the United States is able to meet the demand of its citizens for power and electricity. This reality requires that we continue to use fossil fuels as we move toward using solely renewable energy.

A significant amount of money and economic gain is to be had from leading on alternative and renewable energy. Some may not care whether or not the Earth is experiencing climate change, but they certainly are in favor of economic opportunities. They can be convinced that the actions of protecting the planet are ones that are green . . . when it comes to making money.

The example of Denmark is but one case of innovation that has had a positive economic and environmental impact. Innovation offers us the best opportunity to combat climate change. The Democratic Party's idea of taxing people and organizations because they pollute is not going to be an incentive to not emit carbon emissions—when has a tax ever been considered an incentive?—but it is a way to tick off Americans. Additionally, if the United States were to somehow implement a program of taxing carbon-emitting sources, there is zero guarantee that these reductions would even make a difference, as other nations would not be bound to these standards.

China, who is a major contributor of pollutants and carbon emissions, does not have any interest in reducing its carbon footprint without having a viable alternative to fall back on. Doing so would mean that it would suffer dire economic consequences. It is the same situation with countries throughout the world. We need to ask ourselves what it is that would move countries like China to embrace technologies and practices that do not negatively impact the environment.

The greatest American exports are not its cars, cigarettes, baseball, clothing, or other commercial products. The truly top American export is its culture. As the United States has emerged as a dominant force around the world and become the world's sole superpower, it has become the prime influencer in determining what is considered to be cool and not cool.

Pop culture is something that we can use to further the United States' efforts to combat climate change. No, this is not a suggestion that we use pop culture to spread the message about the three Rs, Reduce, Reuse, Recycle. What we can do is make American products, particularly those that are the result of innovation, be desirable and cool.

(Yes, this quite possibly is one of the less intelligent-sounding sentences in this entire book.)

What is meant by making positive and pro-environmental products cool is creating a consumer demand for them. If Chinese consumers were to replace their existing cars with electric cars manufactured by Tesla, for example, a positive impact on the environmental would certainly be noted.

Republican elected officials who embrace the notion of climate change are subject to being targeted come a primary election. In 2010, Bob Inglis, a Republican congressman from South Carolina was defeated in the Republican primary. Other elements contributed to his defeat, as Inglis is more of a moderate Republican, but climate change was the primary reason that he lost.

After leaving the House of Representatives, Inglis began working toward reducing the impact of climate change. Today, he advocates for solutions:

> We need a pivot from the right toward a conversation about solutions. Conservatives have recoiled in disputation of climate science because the proffered solutions are anathema. Cap-and-trade for carbon emissions won't work the way it worked for acid rain. The Clean Power Plan is a regulatory quagmire. Conservatives can't embrace those solutions, but they can step forward with other solutions that fit with bedrock principles of free enterprise.
>
> Those solutions? Eliminate all subsidies for all fuels. Make all fuels fully accountable for all of the costs they bring upon society. Figure a way to make it in our trading partners' interests to join us on a level playing field where all products bear all of their climate costs. No more socializing soot. No more passing on climate costs to future generations.[86]

All of this is easier said than done. There will be stiff headwinds in making this a tenet of the Republican Party, as there will be those that view it as a sort of heresy or betrayal of what we stand for. This is because Democrats have been incredibly successful at politicizing the environmental issue. Instead of wanting the country to come together and unite to do the common good, they sought to find ways to score political points. Of course, in order to receive the spoils of victory, there must be a loser and Republicans were made into such.

Another argument is to be made in favor of reducing the impact of climate change. Let's remember the impact of Hurricane Sandy. New York City and New Jersey were heavily impacted by the October 2012 storm. Homes were made unlivable, businesses were wiped away, tourism was negatively impacted, and infrastructure was severely damaged. The total cost of Hurricane Sandy is estimated to be approximately $65 billion.[87]

The cost of Hurricane Sandy is still rising. New York City is taking years to recover and repair the infrastructure, particularly its public transit system. The New York City subway system is still damaged with parts being systematically taken off-line for extended periods of time—in some cases a few years—to be repaired. (Salt water and subway tracks do not mix.)

So how in the heck is Hurricane Sandy connected to climate change? Sandy was a brutal storm that was fed by rising sea levels that were caused by climate change. It hammered New York and New Jersey and wreaked havoc wherever it landed. It is highly probable that another storm will hit a major metropolitan area and cause significant damage. This next storm most likely will not be as powerful as Hurricane Sandy, but rising sea levels make it easier for coastal waters to overflow and significant flooding to occur. We must not forget that most tunnels between Brooklyn and the island of Manhattan were flooded by Hurricane Sandy (both subway and vehicular tunnels). The Hudson River wound up setting a record, seeing water levels rise to over thirteen feet high.[88] This eclipsed the previous record of ten feet, which was set more than fifty years prior.

The cost of the damage that these types of storms can cause is too high to bear again. If the United States were to routinely have to deal with the economic impact of storms enhanced by climate change, we would be in serious trouble. Additionally, metropolitan areas cannot afford to spend years recovering from disasters. What would happen if Washington, DC had its subway tunnels flooded and the subway tracks damaged? Or if it occurred in Boston, Houston, or some other American city? Reducing the risk of this happening will cost money, but it certainly will cost less than repairing the damage for a disaster that could have been prevented.

The infrastructure of the United States has been crumbling for years, but efforts to fix it have met resistance. The consequences of this neglect of key infrastructure can be seen in Flint, Michigan, where residents were drinking contaminated water for months. This could have been avoided had Michigan and Flint done the right thing by replacing Flint's water pipes long ago. Instead, they chose to let that aging infrastructure deteriorate to the point that it was poisoning the very people it was supposed to provide clean drinking water to. Now, this willful inaction could end up costing the State of Michigan millions of dollars in claims stemming from lawsuits.[89] That is not good, either fiscally or morally.

Let's be honest here: the prospect of spending money to repair key infrastructure is something that neither Republicans nor Democrats really want to do. Few voters think of it in a positive light, as in their view, the infrastructure is working just fine today. They are blissfully unaware that our infrastructure is on the brink of collapse.

However, this is another example of how we must spend some money now in order to avoid paying a lot more money in the future. Think of it as an investment. Water pipes and water mains are old and decrepit. They are disintegrating to the point that they are poisoning the water that Americans are drinking. Sure, we could continue the approach of crossing our fingers and hoping for the best—as no money needs to be spent provided nothing bad happens. However this strategy implodes the moment things go south. It ends up costing the state and local governments a great deal of money to not only fix the problem, but in the lawsuits that follow.

Issues such as this require that Republicans stand up and speak hard truths that voters will not like to hear. The need to spend in order to protect from future calamity is very real. We cannot afford to hope and pray that bad things do not happen, or to continue making choices that feel good in the short-term but only make things worse in the long run instead. Sure, replacing key environmental infrastructure and helping to foster increased use of reusable and clean energy is not terribly sexy. It may not lead to the next big invention such as the iPhone, but it is absolutely necessary for the Earth and for reversing the view that the Republican Party is anti-science.

Chapter 15
To 2018 and beyond!

THE REPUBLICAN PARTY IS AT A PIVOTAL MOMENT IN ITS HISTORY. Our fragile coalition of Tea Party conservatives, economic conservatives, social conservatives, and neoconservatives has clearly ruptured. The 2016 election and the election cycle that follows will be a battle for the soul of the party. What faction shall emerge on top and what direction the party shall take are anybody's guess. Many voters seek to end what they perceive to be the cause for their ills and who they feel are betrayers—the establishment. They believe that the establishment has wronged them and it is high time that they be punished. Such punishment, these disenfranchised Americans believe, should come in the form of burning the entire thing to the ground.

It certainly is time for the Republican Party to take a good look in the mirror and figure out where it wants to go from here and what it wants to be. Many younger Republicans view this schism that has developed among the differing GOP factions as the perfect opportunity for a rebranding and rebuilding. It is appropriate that we embrace chance to renovate ourselves and make the Republican Party stronger.

I am worried about the impact of Donald Trump's presidential campaign on the Republican Party as a whole. His campaign has only made it tougher for Republicans to fix their damaged image among millennials and urban residents. Trump's hateful rhetoric and policies are not in sync with the values of conservatives and the Republican Party. His campaign has been covered by the press with every utterance or bout of verbal diarrhea receiving 24/7 coverage from breathless commentators and reporters. So highlighted was his campaign that by mid-March 2016, it was calculated that the broadcast networks had given Trump over $1.8 billion worth of free airtime. The media certainly were the enablers of the Trump candidacy and deserve a portion of the blame for his popularity.

Such saturation coverage of a candidate with so many flaws only helped to reinforce the caricature that Trump and his unhinged actions were making the Republican Party out to be.

After the 2016 election, Republicans face an even tougher task of rebuilding the party, establishing itself in urban areas, and connecting with millennials. Donald Trump's campaign has inflicted damage by making all Republicans appear to be anti-immigrant, foulmouthed, anti-Muslim, pro–mocking the disabled, pro–imperial presidency, lacking in compassion, and misogynistic. Each and every one of these things that Trump has done has made it so that Republicans will have to stand up and say, "Donald Trump does not represent the values of the Republican Party."

In February 2016's South Carolina Republican primary, Donald Trump won every voting demographic save one: millennials.[90] This adds even greater concern about where the Republican Party is going with millennials. A December 2015 poll found that only 17.5 percent of Americans aged eighteen through twenty-four viewed Trump in a positive light. In this same poll, it was found that when it came to independents that were aged eighteen through twenty-four, a majority of 62 percent viewed Trump in a negative light versus 14 percent who viewed him in a positive one.[91] These younger millennials are allowing Donald Trump and his views to represent the views of the Republican Party. This does not bode well for the future of the GOP and its representatives.

The Republican Party is a party that believes in small and limited government. We believe in the dignity and rights of the individual citizen. We believe in ensuring that our military is strong and able to confront any threat that confronts us. We believe in reforming entitlement programs so that they will survive and serve Americans. We believe in providing our kids with the best education possible so that they can climb the ladder of opportunity. We believe in having the executive branch rule not by executive order, but through the approval of the Congress. We believe in ensuring that the economy is strong and fair for all. Our list of beliefs goes on and on, and you presumably don't want to be bored to tears by it. So, know this: we believe in conservative values (smaller government, individual liberty, pro-family policies, pro-growth policies, and letting local governments take the lead), many of which are woven throughout the ideas promoted in this book.

Where the Republican Party goes after the 2016 election depends on its actual outcome. Could the GOP presidential nominee take the White House? Will they get millennials and urban voters engaged to the point that their vote makes a difference? What about Hillary Clinton? The answers to these questions and more will be answered on Election Day 2016. Then, it is up to the Republican Party to take these answers and build for future elections.

There are several scenarios that could play out on November 8, 2016. If Donald Trump were to receive the 270 or more required electoral votes to become the forty-fifth president of the United States, this could actually forestall the party's transition to a more millennial- and urban-based recruitment policy. Let's be clear; there is nothing more important than defeating Hillary Clinton and taking back the White House in 2016. However, a GOP victory would make it harder for some within the party to see the course that must be taken in order to win over millennials and urban voters. "If it ain't broke don't fix" it will be the logic of resistance. Yet, what is clear is that the wheel of future progress is clearly breaking down. The stresses being placed on the current GOP voters will become greater and greater with each passing year as many factors work to reduce the size of the base. There could very well be a fight between the old guard of the Republican Party and voices that recognize that millennials are the future. It might not be a fight we want, but it is a fight that will be worth having.

Another outcome of 2016 would be a Hillary Clinton victory. This, which would be the third straight presidential election that a Democrat has won the White House, will cause the party to continue its soul-searching. A small and vocal group of Republicans will passionately argue that we must get even more conservative and never compromise. Adopting such a tactic and viewpoint would further hasten the GOP's decline and problems winning elections. Given the potential for this particular group to hyperventilate and divorce itself from reality, we will need to be prepared for vocal opposition to moving the Republican Party toward the future.

As outlined throughout this book, there are ways in which we can approach multiple issues that will allow the Republican Party to build its supporters and base, which in turn will enable electoral victories in the future. The Republican Party must, for lack of a better term, grow a pair and invest in urban areas. Sure, they will see more than their fair share of opposition and setbacks. We have a large amount of hurdles, many of our own making. Many, particularly the old guard of the Republican Party, will view this effort as the equivalent of a car being stuck in the mud. The driver keeps trying to get the car moving by giving the car gas, but the wheels just spin in place.

The reality is that this car is not stuck in the mud. It actually is climbing a mountain. At the base of the mountain the incline is quite steep, but as the mountain rises, the incline decreases and the resistance encountered on the way up is lessened. The key is being willing to endure the difficult beginning of the endeavor.

Democrats have a massive electoral advantage in presidential elections. Starting off with 104 electoral votes from California, Illinois, and New York is a huge boon to the Democratic Party's presidential nominee. Not only do they get 38.5 percent of the electoral votes required to win the presidential race, but they don't have to do anything to earn them. No, Democrats don't spend any money, time, or effort to get these. They can save these resources to fight the Republican presidential nominee in swing states. Many of these swing states used to be reliably GOP voting states. Now, Democrats are licking their lips as they put Republicans on the defensive in many of them.

Virginia, North Carolina, Colorado, Nevada, Iowa, and New Mexico all are battlegrounds that Democrats have pushed from being "red states" to "purple states." This didn't happen overnight. Because the Republicans were no longer challenging Democrats in urban areas, the Democrats didn't have to spend money and resources defending their home turf. Instead, they took these savings and decided to put the GOP on the defensive in areas where it was previously strong. This started in the 1990s and became electorally successful in 2008 when Barack Obama shifted the electoral landscape. Obama won Virginia, North Carolina, Iowa, Nevada, Colorado, New Mexico, Indiana, Iowa, and New Hampshire. In 2012, all of these states, with the exception of Indiana and North Carolina, again went blue and voted for Barack Obama over Mitt Romney. Each and every one of them are viewed as toss-up states for the 2016 election as well.

These are all states that the Democratic Party targeted, established a beachhead in, and then slowly built up a presence that moved the electorate. What states has the Republican Party done this same thing to? None.

Of course, the old guard of the GOP will adhere to their misguided belief that any move to promote the Republican Party in Democratic areas would be a waste of time, money, and resources. They will say that the only measure of success would be if we turned a state like New York into a reliable Republican state. Obviously, this would be a wonderful achievement for the Republican Party, but let's be realists here: it isn't likely to happen for at least twenty years. What can happen is the following:

1. By challenging them on their home turf, Republicans will force Democrats to expend precious resources in defending their electoral strongholds. These resources would otherwise be used by Democrats to win in swing states.
2. Republicans would make headway with voting blocs that they have not previously targeted. While not acquiring a majority of them, African American and Hispanic voters would move away from the Democratic Party and toward the Republican Party. This would help to kill charges that the GOP doesn't care about minority voters.
3. Given time, the targeted states would become swing states. This would lessen the burden on the Republican Party in states like Virginia and North Carolina that have moved from red to purple. They would be able to revert to red.

Sadly, at least for the old guard of the Republican Party, this strategy would divert money from their pockets and are counter to their operating philosophy. Again, many of these old guard consultants and operatives have shed their idealism and have begun to view campaigns and elections as opportunities to make as much money as possible. This does not help the Republican Party and its goals of growing throughout the country. Campaigns are a battle of ideas that put each side on the offensive. They are not defensive pushes designed to hold onto power.

Another problem with the old guard is that it believes the old adage that as younger voters get older, they will become more conservative. This approach is a fundamental miscalculation. All of the data points to this not happening with millennials. In their eyes, the GOP brand is a thing of the past and holds no appeal because it just doesn't target them. The same is true with urban and minority voters.

One aspect of this growth of the Republican Party has been intentionally overlooked throughout this entire book. Purposefully ignored has been the question of what type of person should be carrying this message to millennials and urban voters. What should this person's background be? How old? Ethnicity? Sure, we could spend a chapter or two discussing who among the Republican ranks should rise to lead the party in the future, but that is counter to our own ideals. Our leaders should emerge naturally, not because somebody wrote that John Smith is the right guy for the right time. Leaders need to rise because their ideas and what they stand for resonate with the public.

Right now, we see that some generation Xers are in position to provide a vital bridge between older generations and millennials. Senator Ben Sasse of Nebraska is one of them. Sasse is forty-four and has served in the United States Senate since 2015. He personally tweets from his own Twitter account, something that few elected officials are willing to do, and is in touch with what is going on in society. If you met Senator Sasse on the street, you would think that he was just a regular guy who liked sports, beer, and pop culture. He's relatable and incredibly intelligent. Where Sasse made his mark in the senate was his maiden floor speech. In that speech, he proceeded to outline the problem with the legislative branch. It perfectly encapsulated the views of the American public of Congress:

> But please do not misunderstand: do not confuse a deliberate approach with passivity. I ran because I think that the public is right that we as a people are not tackling the generational crises that we face: we don't have a long-term foreign policy for the age of jihad and cyber-war; our entitlement budgets are completely fake; we are entering an age where work and

> jobs will be more fundamentally disrupted than at any point since hunter-gatherers first settled in agrarian villages. And yet we don't really have any plans. I think the public is right that we as a Congress are not shepherding the country through the serious debates we must have about the future of this great nation.

Sasse continued:

> And if I can be brutally honest for a moment: I'm home basically every weekend, and what I hear—and what I'm sure most of you hear—is some version of this: a pox on both parties and all your houses. We don't believe politicians are even trying to fix this mess. To the Republicans, to those who claim this new majority is leading the way: few believe that. To the grandstanders who use this institution as a platform for outside pursuits: few believe the country's needs are as important to you as your ambitions. To the Democrats, who did this body harm through nuclear tactics: few believe bare-knuckled politics are a substitute for principled governing. And does anyone doubt that many on both the right and the left now salivate for more of these radical tactics? The people despise us all. And why is this? Because we're not doing the job we were sent here to do. The Senate isn't tackling the great national problems that worry those we work for.[92]

This speech of Senator Sasse's was no accident. Poll after poll has clearly shown that the American people view politicians as favorably as they do stepping in dog poop. Millennials take an especially dim view of politicians and Sasse's speech was one that they could listen to and say, "Hey, this guy gets why I am pissed off and frustrated." Millennials are incredibly disappointed with the action (or inaction) of Congress.[93] It turns them off to the political process and makes them see it as a waste of time. That is not what we want it to be and nor should it ever be seen as such.

So who should we have as the voices of the Republican Party among millennials and urban voters? In truth, few people would fit the bill at present. Congresswoman Elise Stefanik (R-New York) is one candidate to be one of the new breed of millennial Republicans. She does not represent a major urban center, as her district is in upstate New York, but she is a millennial who at age thirty became the youngest woman ever elected to Congress in 2014. Like Senator Sasse, Representative Stefanik is in touch with the frustrations and feelings of millennials across the nation.

Yet, Stefanik cannot count any fellow Republican members of Congress as being fellow millennials. She stands alone in the halls of Capitol Hill. Yes, there are millennial Republicans in Congress, but they are all staffers. Stefanik is the unicorn. This requires that we bring in new blood to the ranks of our federally-elected officials. These new representatives and senators must be millennials, of course. It would be even better if they were urban millennials, but that is a tall order considering the status or lack thereof of the GOP in urban areas. They will be the people that will help push the Republican Party to where it needs to be both in strategy and policy. Additionally, these millennial Republican-elected officials will offer a bridge to the millennial and urban communities. They know how to speak to these key constituencies and will prove quite valuable as we seek to expand the Republican Party.

Until we have these millennials elected to the House of Representatives and the United States Senate, the GOP will have to rely on the leadership of Republican elected officials that are just a few years too old to be considered millennials. Senator Tom Cotton, Representative Justin Amash, Representative Adam Kinzinger, Representative Lee Zeldin, and Representative Jaime Herrera Beutler are all in their mid- to late thirties and represent their districts/states in the halls of Congress. Of course, we must also count Senator Ben Sasse as one of these young leaders of the Republican Party, too.

The very things that Senator Sasse railed against in his maiden floor speech are the very things that the old guard of the Republican Party want to promote. Millennials and urban voters are not people that these consultants care about winning over. Why should we keep them in the driver's seat of where the Republican Party should go? They have demonstrated that they do not understand or particularly value millennials. Additionally, they have failed to properly embrace the technology and platforms required to speak to a millennial or to a connected audience. Instead, they stick to the outdated tradition of reaching voters using methods and technologies that are in decline. Continuing down this path is a recipe for failure at the national level.

Republican pollster Kristen Soltis Anderson made note of how every federal election from 2008 on has traded success:

> Then came the 2010 elections and the significant Republican wave of that year, in which Republicans won a multitude of races across the country. Suddenly it seemed that not all hope was lost for the GOP. The pendulum quickly swung back, of course, and by the 2012 election the Republican "brand image" was worse than ever, with Democrats retaining the White House. Come 2014, we were right back to Republican euphoria, with election victories that lent credence to the theory that it is Democrats who are doomed in the long run because of their declining appeal with a large swath of white working-class voters.[94]

Soltis Anderson gave a very apt description of what happened the past few election cycles. The important lesson to take away from all of these races is that voters have not solidly settled into one side of the aisle or the other. They are vacillating between Republicans and Democrats. Americans are not sold on what the Democratic Party and its candidates are selling, and this means that we have the room to maneuver the Republican Party so that it is something that voters become invested in.

Also true are the claims that the Democratic Party is losing its appeal with working-class white voters. However, this voting bloc is not one that will sustain the Republican Party in the elections to come. In fact, it is a shrinking sector of the population, which is the very reason that there is alarm about the future viability of the GOP at the ballot box.

Bruce Rauner was smart enough to recognize the shifting electoral demographics when he ran for governor of Illinois in 2014. Knowing that he could not win with white working-class voters alone, his campaign wisely targeted urban voters in Cook County. The strategy of utilizing digital platforms to increase the campaign's reach in the traditionally Democratic stronghold of Chicago resulted in Rauner's gubernatorial win. Further, it was the message that Rauner's campaign pushed that resonated with the voters and saw him elected governor. Had he not had a message that resonated with Chicago's voting population, all of his efforts would have been for naught. It is important to remember that you can have the best system for speaking to voters, but if you do not have a good message to deliver, then you are wasting time and money.

Thankfully, some Republican officials and operatives recognize this. Each day, they fight for their voices to be heard. They see how millennials and urban voters are not buying what conservatives are selling, and they, like me, are worried. They have the foresight to see that not evolving who we are as a party and what we stand for is no longer working. We must modernize with the times but without sacrificing our conservative values.

Adapting and evolving for the times is not something to fear, but it should be something that we embrace. Doing so shows that the Republican Party is a modern party and not a group of people yearning for the "good old days" that are way behind us. Millennials and urban voters are the future of the party, whether we like it or not. Embracing this fact is the key to moving forward and being able to win over these voting blocs. Remember, the 2010 US Census found that urban residents compose over 80 percent of the population of the United States. We can't win by alienating or ignoring those 250 plus million Americans and focusing on less than 20 percent of the population of the United States. It is electoral suicide.

Baby boomers and rural residents are a shrinking sector of the United States' population, while millennials and urban residents are a growing sector of the United States' population. Ignoring them will see only tougher elections and increased electoral defeats. Without winning races and putting the Republican Party's candidates in office, there is no way that we can use our conservative policies to help the United States of America.

It is important to remember that millennials and urban voters must be viewed as more than just a vote or tool that ensures party relevancy. Republicans must see them as necessary for our long-term success. In turn, they must see us as necessary for their own triumphs. Furthermore, millennials and urban voters must hold Republicans accountable for their promises on the campaign trail. Should we fail to deliver on promised reforms and outreach, minorities, millennials, and other urban residents have every reason to once again not take the Republican Party and its leaders seriously. If we move on a path that veers away from issues and policies that resonate with these sectors of the electorate and return to the very things that have caused our diminished standing with these groups, then our problems of today will once again become the problems of tomorrow.

The Republican Party's goals are to provide opportunity and the path to it for all Americans. While the onus to take that path is on the citizen, we can and must make it as easy and navigable as possible. That is how we bring millennials and urban residents into the Republican Party and change how they view us as a party. We can no longer afford to be viewed as old-fashioned, behind the times, and damaged. That will not help us win at the ballot box every November. In fact, each subsequent election will see our base grow smaller and smaller until it ultimately becomes too small to field a strong result. When this happens, we will be forced to do what has been recommended in this book. The only difference is that we will be several years behind and face an even tougher climb out of the hole that we have dug for ourselves.

We have the opportunity to reach out to millennials and urban voters. We have the opportunity to grow and reach these voters that do not trend toward us, but would if we work hard to earn their trust. We have the opportunity to claim urban areas as Republican strongholds. We have the opportunity to beat Democrats on their home turf. We have the opportunity to build the party for the future.

Let us go forth and change the way we are viewed—countering the left and the media's caricature of Republicans, combined with communicating our conservative values to them in the clearest and best medium possible. Our values and ideas can help millions of Americans, but we must first be in the urban areas that we seek to help and to promote ideas that are palatable.

The problem of our shrinking base exists. There can be no doubt about that. We do not have the trust and required standing in the minds of millennials and urban Americans in order to earn their votes. Now it is time for Republicans to deal with this challenge and build for the future by communicating our ideas through means and mediums that our target audience will actually use. This means talking to millennials on the devices they use.

In its white paper/report, "Millennials come of age," Experian Marketing Services highlighted the significant amount of time that millennials spend on smartphones:

> Seventy-seven percent of all millennials and 83 percent of millennial cell phone owners have a smartphone today. And on average millennial smartphone owners spend about 14.5 hours a week—just over two hours a day—using their phones. In fact, millennials spend so much time on their smartphones that they account for 41 percent the total time

> that Americans spend using smartphones, despite making up just 29 percent of the population. During a typical week, millennial smartphone owners in aggregate spend 765.9 million hours talking, texting, accessing social media, etc. on their smartphones, more than any other generation.[95]

Experian Marketing Service's findings confirm that Republicans need to reach millennials where they congregate. On social media, through texts, on the apps they use on their phones, etc.

Increasingly, millennials are turning away from consuming information and media from traditional resources. They are not watching cable news, nor are they buying newspapers or magazines. Instead, they choose what information they want to consume and do so by using the mediums they choose. These mediums are the Internet, streaming video, and other digital sources.

The groan of the old guard and bean counters who read the prior paragraph is audible. They read the previous paragraph and they see a call for putting money into a communications strategy that is somewhat foreign to them and will take away from the budgets of other communications strategies. They see it as taking away from television advertising budgets, because everybody watches television, right?

The simple answer is no, they do not. More and more Americans are choosing to "cut the cord" and not receive cable or satellite television. It is estimated that by 2018, one in five households in the United States will not have cable television.

> Cable and satellite providers will steadily lose customers through 2019. The number of US households subscribing to cable TV will drop 0.4 percent this year, while the number of US households subscribing to satellite TV will drop 1.5 percent.[96]

As a result of this trend in American consumer behavior, we can calm the nerves and allay the fears of the bean counters and old guard by showing them that changing the "where we talk" to voters does not necessitate spending more money or taking away from another platform, such as television. In fact, it could very well mean that we save money. Remember, the cost of placing an ad on television is far greater than running a targeted advertisement online. Plus, the results of targeted digital advertisements are far greater than those of television campaigns.

Look at how companies are spending their advertising budgets now. Magna Global has projected that digital ad spending will eclipse traditional ad spending in 2016.

> Digital media spending has been booming as advertisers increasingly pour ad dollars into social and video formats, as well as search ads, to keep up with changing consumption habits. At the same time, advertisers have been pulling back on their investment in most types of traditional media categories, including television.[97]

Like the George W. Bush presidential campaign did in the 2000 election, the Republican Party should look to the private sector to see the future. In 2000 and 2004, it was microtargeting. Now in 2016 and on, it is digital advertising, which is overtaking television and traditional advertising.

The party that is dominant in the digital realm will have a leg up on winning over millennials in the coming election cycles. Republicans are equipped to be that party, but we must also recognize that we will have more work to do than Democrats. We are at a disadvantage, as millennials are now naturally skeptical of Republicans and their policies. Yet, there is hope. We have great ideas that can produce results that millennials and urban voters will like and cheer.

Where we go as a party is up to us and us alone. The Republican Party controls its own destiny and can choose whether or not it withers and declines or survives and thrives. The key to our future success lies with millennials, the largest segment of the population in the United States. It also lies with urban voters, who, according to the United States Census Bureau, are over 80 percent of the United States population.

For those who still are on the fence as to whether or not this undertaking is worthwhile, consider this: Democrats rely on these voting blocs in order to stay in power and perpetuate their well-meaning, but deeply misguided policies. We have seen the results achieved by Democrats who are placed in charge of urban areas, and these results have not made America's cities better places. They face problems of equality, problems of education, problems of crime, problems of economics, and many more. Now think about what would happen if we were to deny Democrats in what is—in their own minds—their home turf?

There are those in politics who view it as more of a contest and blood sport that allows only one side to be the victor and the other to be the loser. So, Republicans defeating Democrats with the votes of millennials and in urban areas election after election would offer those on the Republican side immense satisfaction while it would be crushing for those on the Democratic side. But let's be frank with one another; this book was not written for the sake of punching Democrats in the nose.

The true reason it was written should have been evident from the start. This book was written because Republicans have a path to winning in the future, but it is a path that some are reluctant to take or simply just don't know how to begin the journey. It might be a long journey, but it will be worthwhile.

Republicans winning in urban areas and with millennials is something that can be done. We will succeed by promoting marriage equality. We will succeed by being pro-science and combating climate change. We will succeed by using conservative ideas to ensure social justice. We will succeed on issues of education. We will succeed by helping to remove debt from the lives of Americans.

We will succeed with pro-family policies. We will succeed by championing Internet freedom. We will succeed on the Second Amendment. We will succeed by fixing entitlement programs and the national debt. We will succeed by fixing our broken immigration system. Finally, we will succeed on matters of foreign policy and national security.

Now the question is, what are we waiting for? Let's get started on this worthwhile endeavor and build the Republican Party for the future. Millennials and urban residents are waiting to be brought into the fold. We have some work to do.

Notes

1 Janet Hook, "Millennial Wave Unsettles Presidential Race," *Wall Street Journal*, February 15, 2016
2 Kelsey Harkness, "Conservatives: Democrat Policies Have Hurt Black Communities," *Daily Signal*, February 11, 2016
3 Chris Edwards, "Obama's Budget: Spending Too High, But Bush Was Worse," CATO Institute, April 10, 2013 http://www.cato.org/blog/obamas-budget-spending-too-high-bush-was-worse
4 Meredith Warren, "The Democrats Stoke Class Warfare," *Boston Globe*, Sept. 10, 2015
5 Bernie Sanders, "The War on the Middle Class," *Boston Globe*, June 12, 2015
6 *Congressional Record*, 110/1, p. H10044
7 Transcript of Ben Carson Interview on CNN's "New Day," March 5, 2015
8 H.R. 1786, 114th Congress, First Session, introduced April 14, 2015
9 Charles C.W. Cooke, *The Conservatarian Manifesto*. New York: Crown Forum, 2015
10 Byron York, "Dems Are Earmark Junkies But GOP Goes Straight," *Examiner*, December 17, 2010 http://archives.sfexaminer.com/sanfrancisco/dems-are-earmark-junkies-but-gop-goes-straight/Content?oid=2166425

11 John Klingner, "Chicago's $63 Billion Debt Burden," *Illinois Policy*, May 12, 2014 https://www.illinoispolicy.org/chicagos-63-billion-debt-burden/

12 Tom Tancredo and John Suthers, "Point/Counterpoint: Marijuana Legalization Amendment," *Colorado Springs Gazette*, September 21, 2012

13 Poll, "Mayor de Blasio's Job Approval Inches Up, Quinnipiac University Poll Finds; Kelly More Effective Than Bratton, But Trails de Blasio," Quinnipiac University, January 19, 2016

14 Richard Fry and Jeffrey S. Passel, "In Post-Recession Era, Young Adults Drive Continuing Rise in Multi-Generational Living," Pew Research Center, July 17, 2014 http://www.pewsocialtrends.org/2014/07/17/in-post-recession-era-young-adults-drive-continuing-rise-in-multi-generational-living/

15 "FAQs," *U.S. Census Bureau*, (FAQ5971) https://ask.census.gov/faq.php?id=5000&faqId=5971

16 Aaron Blake, "How Urban Voters Failed Democrats in 2014," *Washington Post*, November 12, 2014

17 Leslie Wayne, "With Microtargeting, Democrats Take Page From Their Rival's Playbook," *The New York Times*, October 31, 2008

18 Claire Cain Miller, "How Obama's Internet Campaign Changed Politics," *The New York Times'* Bit Blog, November. 7, 2008 http://bits.blogs.nytimes.com/2008/11/07/how-obamas-internet-campaign-changed-politics/?_r=0

19 Zoe Fox, "The Digital Smackdown: Obama 2008 vs. Obama 2012," Mashable, Sept. 23, 2012, http://mashable.com/2012/09/23/obama-digitial-comparison/

20 Maggie Haberman and Alexander Burns, "Romney's Fail Whale: ORCA The Vote-Tracker Left Team 'Flying Blind,'" *Politico*'s Burns & Haberman blog, November 8, 2012 http://www.politico.com/blogs/burns-haberman/2012/11/romneys-fail-whale-orca-the-vote-tracker-left-team-flying-blind-updated-149098

21 *National Charter School Study*. Center for Research on Education Outcomes: Stanford University, 2013

22 Howard Blume, "California Voters Take a Dim View of Teacher Tenure," *Los Angeles Times*, April 11, 2015

23 Cecilia Kang, "Bridging a Digital Divide That Leaves School Children Behind," *The New York Times*, February 22, 2016

24 "Millennials: Our Newest Generation in Higher Education," Northern Illinois University: Faculty Development and Instructional Design Center

25 Press Release, "$78.5 Million Settlement in Whistleblower Lawsuit Against University of Phoenix," Lief Cabraser Heimann & Bernstein LLP, Dec. 14, 2009

26 Erin El Issa, "2015 American Household Credit Card Debt Study," NerdWallet, https://www.nerdwallet.com/blog/credit-card-data/average-credit-card-debt-household/

27 Blake Neff, "The 9 Most Preposterous Parts of Melissa Click's Absurd Resume," *Daily Caller*, November 10, 2015 http://dailycaller.com/2015/11/10/the-9-most-preposterous-parts-of-melissa-clicks-absurd-resume/

28 Evan Feinberg, "Heavily In Debt Millennials Now Must Foot The Federal Deficit Bill Too," *Forbes*, October 18, 2013

29 Mark Knoller, "National Debt Has Increased More Under Obama Than Under Bush," *CBS News*, March 19, 2012 http://www.cbsnews.com/news/national-debt-has-increased-more-under-obama-than-under-bush/

30 Dave Boyer, "$20 Trillion Man: National Debt Nearly Doubles During Obama Presidency," *Washington Times*, November 1, 2015

31 Chris Edwards Testimony Before Committee on Budget, United States House of Representatives, "The Need to Balance the Budget and Reduce Federal Debt," submitted June 17, 2015

32 "2015 Federal Budget in Pictures," The Heritage Foundation, http://www.heritage.org/federalbudget/budget-entitlement-programs

33 "2015 Federal Budget in Pictures," The Heritage Foundation, http://www.heritage.org/federalbudget/entitlements-historical-tax-levels

34 "Angry Silents, Disengaged Millenials: The Generation Gap and the 2012 Election," Pew Research Center, November 3, 2011

35 Phil Galewitz, "Study: Nearly A Third of Doctors Won't See New Medicaid Patients," Kaiser Health News, August 6, 2012, http://khn.org/news/third-of-medicaid-doctors-say-no-new-patients/

36 Kym Hymowitz, "How Should Conservatives Think about Family Leave?," *National Review*, January 21, 2015

37 "The Staggering Rise in Elder Care Costs," *Associated Press*, April 10, 2015

38 Liz O'Donnell, "The Crisis Facing America's Working Daughters," *Atlantic*, February 9, 2016

39 "The MetLife Study of Caregiving Costs to Working Caregivers," MetLife, June 2011

40 Margeurite Reardon, "FCC Opens Hot-Button Net Neutrality Proposal For Public Debate," *CNET*, May 15, 2014 http://www.cnet.com/news/fcc-opens-controversial-net-neutrality-proposal-up-for-debate/

41 Alex Wilhelm and Sarah Buhr, "FCC Passes Strict Net Neutrality Regulations On 3-2 Vote," *TechCrunch*, February 26, 2015 http://techcrunch.com/2015/02/26/fcc-passes-strict-net-neutrality-regulations-on-3-2-vote

42 Press Release, "CES 2016: Full-Page Ad Targets FCC Chairman Wheeler's Attacks on Internet Freedom," Jan. 6, 2016

43 Patricia Cartes, "Announcing the Twitter Trust & Safety Council," February 9, 2016 https://blog.twitter.com/2016/announcing-the-twitter-trust-safety-council

44 Alex Pfeiffer, "Twitter Users Can Report Tweets 'In Disagreement With My Opinion,'" *Daily Caller*, February 25, 2016 http://dailycaller.com/2016/02/25/twitter-users-can-report-tweets-in-disagreement-with-my-opinion/

45 Evan Feinberg, "Millennials to the FCC: 'Don't Break the Internet' Commentary," *Roll Call*, September 22, 2014
46 Doug Aamoth, "John Oliver's Net Neutrality Rant Crashes FCC Servers," *Time*, June 3, 2014
47 Texas v. Johnson, 491 U.S. 397, p. 415
48 "Poll: New Yorkers Favor Uber in Regulatory Battle," *NY1 News*, August 10, 2015
49 Errol Louis, "How Uber Saved Me From Cabs: Mayor de Blasio is Leaving N.Y.ers Stranded—Like a Black Man Trying to Hail a Taxi Uptown," *New York Daily News*, July 21, 2015
50 Andrew Tangel and Josh Dawsey, "Report: Uber Hasn't Worsened NYC Traffic," *Wall Street Journal*, January 14, 2016
51 John B. Horrigan and Maeve Duggan, "Home Broadband 2015," Pew Research Center, December 21, 2015
52 Claire Groden, "New York City Launches Free Wi-Fi Hotspots," *Fortune Magazine*, February 21, 2016
53 Ashley Carman, "Hillary Clinton Pledges Broadband for all Americans in $275 Billion Infrastructure plan," *The Verge*, December 1, 2015 http://www.theverge.com/2015/12/1/9826962/hillary-clinton-infrastructure-internet-plan
54 Maggie Fox, "Obamacare Website Fails as Deadline Arrives," *NBC News*, March 31, 2014 http://www.nbcnews.com/storyline/obamacare-deadline/obamacare-website-fails-deadline-arrives-n67666
55 Harry McCracken, "How Google and HUD Plan to Bring Broadband to More Americans," *FastCompany*, January 7, 2016, https://www.fastcompany.com/3055224/how-google-and-hud-plan-to-bring-broadband-to-more-americans
56 Fox News Sunday: 2007 "Choosing the President" interviews, May 14, 2007
57 Mike Levine and Tom Liddy, "Man Charged With Murder in San Francisco Pier Shooting, DA Says," ABC News, July 6, 2015 http://abcnews.go.com/US/man-charged-murder-san-francisco-pier-shooting-da/story?id=32262378

58 "Steinle Family Announces Lawsuit Against Gov't Agencies in SF Murder," *Fox News*, September 1, 2015 http://www.foxnews.com/politics/2015/09/01/kate-steinle-family-announce-lawsuits-against-agencies-blamed-for-her-murder.html

59 Natalie Johnson, "San Francisco Passes Resolution Upholding Sanctuary Policies Despite Kate Steinle Murder," *Daily Signal*, October 21, 2015 http://dailysignal.com/2015/10/21/san-francisco-passes-resolution-upholding-sanctuary-policies-despite-kate-steinle-murder/

60 Carl Campanile, "New Bill Could Give Illegal Aliens Voting Rights in New York City," *New York Post*, February 22, 2016

61 Robert Tracinski, "Nothing is More 'Conservative' Than Birthright Citizenship," *Federalist*, August 20, 2015 http://thefederalist.com/2015/08/20/nothing-is-more-conservative-than-birthright-citizenship/

62 Peter D. Salins, "The Conservative Case for Legalizing America's Illegal Immigrants," *New York Post*, June 14, 2014

63 Roy Beck, "Why is the Biometric Exit System Still Not in Place," *The Hill*, January 20, 2016 http://thehill.com/blogs/congress-blog/homeland-security/266341-why-is-the-biometric-exit-tracking-system-still-not-in

64 Sara Murray, "Many in U.S. Illegally Overstayed Their Visas," *Wall Street Journal*, April 7, 2013 http://www.wsj.com/articles/SB10001424127887323916304578404960101110032

65 Riley Walters, "2015 Had the Most Terror Plots in the US Since 9/11," *The Daily Signal*, January 13, 2016 http://dailysignal.com/2016/01/13/2015-had-the-most-terror-plots-in-the-us-since-911/

66 "The Generation Gap on Foreign Policy and National Security Issues," Pew Research Center, November 11, 2011 http://www.pewresearch.org/daily-number/the-generation-gap-on-foreign-policy-and-national-security-issues/

67 Aaron Strickland, "How Do Millennials View Foreign Policy?" *Daily Signal*, December 30, 2015 http://dailysignal.com/2015/12/30/how-do-millennials-view-foreign-policy/

68 Richard Haass, "Time to End the North Korean Threat," *Wall Street Journal*, December 23, 2014

69 "Public Continues to Back U.S. Drone Attacks," Pew Research Center, May 28, 2015

70 Peter Bergen and Megan Braun, "Drone is Obama's Weapon of Choice," *CNN*, September 19, 2012 http://www.cnn.com/2012/09/05/opinion/bergen-obama-drone/

71 Allison Lex, "9 Things Invented For Military Use That You Now Encounter in Everyday Life," *Mental Floss*, October 21, 2012 http://mentalfloss.com/article/31510/9-things-invented-military-use-you-now-encounter-everyday-life

72 Charles C.W. Cooke, *The Conservatarian Manifesto*. New York: Crown Forum, 2015

73 Transcript of Republican Presidential Candidates' Debate, August 6, 2015

74 Sean Captain, "The Demographics of Occupy Wall Street," *Fast Company*, October 9, 2011 https://www.fastcompany.com/1789018/demographics-occupy-wall-street

75 Fred Siegel, "The Riot Ideology, Reborn," *City Journal*, Autumn 2015

76 "Information About Student Health Insurance," Office of Research and Graduate Studies, University of Missouri, August 25, 2015, https://gradstudies. missouri.edu/about/news-events/news-features/2015/information-about-student-health-insurance/

77 Transcript of Donald Trump's Interview on Fox News, November 22, 2015

78 Transcript of Gov. Nikki Haley's Speech to the National Press Club, September 2, 2015

79 David A. Graham, "The Death of Jeremy Mardis and the Honesty of the Police," *The Atlantic*, November 12, 2015

80 "Ex-officer, Metro Named in Federal Civil Rights Lawsuit," *Associated Press*, February 9, 2016

81 "MU Chancellor to Confer with Board of Curators about Body Camera Footage of Melissa Click," *Columbia Missourian*, February 14, 2016

82 Transcript of Marco Rubio's Remarks to CNN Town Hall Meeting (Greenville, S.C.), February 17, 2016

83 Eli Lehrer, "Reagan, the Environmentalist," *Weekly Standard*, June 17, 2013 http://www.weeklystandard.com/reagan-the-environmentalist/article/733961

84 Laura Barron-Lopez, "Senate Votes that Climate Change is Real," *The Hill*, January 21, 2015

85 Jamie Lendino, "This Fully Transparent Solar Cell Could Make Every Window and Screen a Power Source," *Extreme Tech*, April 20, 2015 http://www.extremetech.com/extreme/188667-a-fully-transparent-solar-cell-that-could-make-every-window-and-screen-a-power-source

86 Bob Inglis, "Climate Action Demands New Thinking from the Left and Right," *Chicago Tribune*, September 22, 2015

87 Doyle Rice, "Hurricane Sandy, Drought Cost U.S. $100 billion," *USA Today*, January 25, 2015

88 "Impacts of Hurricane Sandy and the Climate Change Connection," World Resources Institute 2012

89 Jennifer Dixon, "Flint lawsuits Could Cost Michigan Taxpayers Millions," *Detroit Free Press*, February 21, 2016

90 Editorial, "Young Voters, Motivated Again," *The New York Times*, February 21, 2016

91 Monmouth College Poll, December 21, 2015

92 *Congressional Record*, 114/1, pp. S7697-7701

93 Asma Khalid, "Generation Disappointed: Millenials Want More From Politics," *NPR*, September 19, 2015 http://www.npr.org/sections/itsallpolitics/2015/09/19/440925347/generation-disappointed-millennials-want-more-from-politics

94 Kristen Soltis Anderson, *The Selfie Vote: Where Millennials are Leading America (and How Republicans Can Keep Up)*, New York: Broadside Books, 2015

95 "Millennials Come of Age," *Experian Marketing Services*, June 2014

96 "Americans Cutting the Cable TV Cord at Increasing Pace," eMarketer December 10, 2015

97 Nathalie Tadena, "Digital Ad Spending in U.S. to Surpass Television Spending in 2016," *Wall Street Journal*, October 15, 2015

Illustration Credits

p. 18 "Chicago's $63 billion debt burden" Illinois Policy Center (May, 2016)

p. 24 "Millennials overtake Baby Boomers as America's largest generation" Pew Research Center, Washington, D.C., (April, 2016) http://www.pewresearch.org/fact-tank/2016/04/25/millennials-overtake-baby-boomers/

p. 36 "How Millennials' political news habits differ from those of Gen Xers and Baby Boomers" Pew Research Center, Washington, D.C., (June, 2015) http://www.pewresearch.org/fact-tank/2015/06/01/political-news-habits-by-generation/

p. 44 Screenshot from barackobama.com

p. 47 Via Twitter.com from @BarackObama

p. 107 "Gun homicide rate down 49% since 1993 peak; public unaware" Pew Research Center, Washington, D.C., (May, 2013) http://www.pewsocialtrends.org/2013/05/07/gun-homicide-rate-down-49-since-1993-peak-public-unaware/

p. 108 "Gun homicide rate down 49% since 1993 peak; public unaware" Pew Research Center, Washington, D.C., (May, 2013) http://www.pewsocialtrends.org/2013/05/07/gun-homicide-rate-down-49-since-1993-peak-public-unaware/

p. 115 "Continued bipartisan support for expanded background checks on gun sales" Pew Research Center, Washington, D.C., (August, 2015) http://www.people-press.org/2015/08/13/continued-bipartisan-support-for-expanded-background-checks-on-gun-sales/

p. 124 "From Germany to Mexico: how America's source of immigrants has changed over a century" Pew Research Center, Washington, D.C., (October, 2015) http://www.pewresearch.org/fact-tank/2015/10/07/a-shift-from-germany-to-mexico-for-americas-immigrants/

p. 150 Copyright © 2015 Gallup, Inc. All rights reserved. The content is used with permission; however, Gallup retains all rights of republication.

p. 151 "61% of young Republicans favor same-sex marriage" Pew Research Center, Washington, D.C., (March, 2014) http://www.pewresearch.org/fact-tank/2014/03/10/61-of-young-republicans-favor-same-sex-marriage/

p. 152 "61% of young Republicans favor same-sex marriage" Pew Research Center, Washington, D.C., (March, 2014) http://www.pewresearch.org/fact-tank/2014/03/10/61-of-young-republicans-favor-same-sex-marriage/

p. 155 "Most U.S. Christian groups grow more accepting of homosexuality" Pew Research Center, Washington, D.C., (December, 2015) http://www.pewresearch.org/fact-tank/2015/12/18/most-u-s-christian-groups-grow-more-accepting-of-homosexuality/

p. 162 Courtesy of Somm Consulting LLC

p. 163 Courtesy of Somm Consulting LLC

p. 179 Courtesy of the University of Texas at Austin McComb's School of Business

p. 180 Courtesy of the University of Texas at Austin McComb's School of Business

p. 181 Courtesy of the University of Texas at Austin McComb's School of Business

Acknowledgments

TO BE HONEST, THERE ARE A MULTITUDE OF PEOPLE AND FRIENDS to thank. First and foremost, I must credit my good friend Steven Beer who encouraged me to write a book. His friendship and guidance over the past few years was instrumental in my professional journey. Next, Dina Fraioli is deserving of extreme thanks, and then some, because of her telling me to pursue the political commentary track just over a year ago. Not only did she recommend I share my thoughts and observations, but Dina gave key advice and helped to open doors that I did not even know existed. They each were major contributors to this book before a single word of it was written.

Of course, my family played a major role, especially during the book's writing. My parents instilled in me the values that I hold dear. They have been a constant source of support in every single thing that I have done. They were always there for me when I needed them to be and set the example of the type of parent I would like to be if and when I have children. They also were happy-ish to help take care of my dog, Rowdy, when writing and work would not permit me to do so. My brother Angus, sister-in-law Liz, their two sons, and my brother Sandy all have been supportive, and I'm glad that they are all in my life. However, for the record, I must reiterate to Liz and Angus that I never signed them up for any political email lists. The accusation is false.

A few friends and colleagues were great resources during the writing of this book. Each provided insight and feedback that were incredibly valuable. Surprisingly, this group was rather bipartisan. So I owe a debt of gratitude to Jerri Ann Henry, Sheril Kirshenbaum, Eric Koch, Nick Iacono, Corey Chambliss, Corey Vale, Nomiki Konst (who helped me figure out the topic of the book and has always been a cheerleader for my efforts), Naveed Jamali, Ben Kissel, Jason Weingartner, Jessica Tarlov, Bethany Mandel, and Michael Kaplan.

Then there were the friends who read the early version of this and could give me their blunt thoughts about how the book was shaping up. Jules and Edda were able to look at my work and give me honest feedback.

Thank you to the friends that tolerated me during the writing period and offered me an escape from the constant writing of my days: Greg, Matt, Henrietta, Michael, Caitlin, Megan, Tatyana, Jonathan, Adrian, Francesca, Daniela, Tim, Biscuit, Rowdy, Sebastian, Cooper, Teresa, Lola, James, Bob, Lauren, Tom, Jeremy, and Andrea.

Joseph Craig and the Skyhorse Publishing team all were a great help in the entire process—especially the editing, as Joe was incredibly patient and insightful.

Also, Peter Zorich and Matthew Siegelheim of Best Guest Media have been a tremendous asset to me for the past year with their efforts to coordinate my television appearances. Not only are they professional, but they are deeply passionate about my success. Additionally, the fantastic team at BGM has been absolutely stellar.

Several people provided wonderful influence, appropriate challenges, guidance and mentorship throughout my life, education, and career. The late Jay Wallberg, whom I miss every single day, taught me to never sweat the small stuff and that laughing your ass off daily is vital. My late uncle Peter was always there when I needed him. The late Judge David G. Trager, Judge Edward

R. Korman, Judge Brian M. Cogan, and Paula Susi each were reliable sources of sound advice. I learned how to write and debate from many teachers throughout my education, but Fordham University's Chris Toulouse really helped me to sharpen my words. His innovative teaching method was the best preparation for a career in the real world.

As I honed my writing craft, several editors were important to my growth as a writer. Seth Mandel, Josh Greenman, Tara Setmayer, Jordan Bloom, Harry Siegel, Nick Powell, and many, many more.

Finally, I must credit the date who rejected me because of my Republican Party membership. I bear her no ill will, but rather must thank her for the honesty and providing me with a great story to tell. Let's just hope she never sees this book and decides to sue me for a portion of the profits.